March 23, 1982

Happy B-Day, Mom!
(& Dad ☺)

Love,
Wendy & Tim

# Betty Crocker's
# Mexican Cookbook

Random House, Inc. New York

# FOREWORD

Welcome to this sampling of Mexican cooking. Lively and surprising in its flavors, colors and textures and offering an abundant variety of ingredients, Mexican cuisine is much more than the popular tortilla, tamale and guacamole.

José Romero, restaurateur and food authority who furnished the recipes in this book, notes that Mexican food commonly found in United States restaurants bears little resemblance to food served in the fine restaurants and private homes of Mexico. It was this discrepancy between ordinary Mexican restaurant fare and its true values that inspired Romero to leave an academic career to open his restaurant, Casa Romero, in Boston's Back Bay. The recipes in this book, like the menu of Casa Romero, specialize in the authentic cuisine of Mexico. All were tested and edited in the Betty Crocker Kitchens for their success and practicality in *your* kitchen.

You will find Mexican food as simple to prepare as that of any other country, and no more time-consuming. All of the ingredients in these recipes or their substitutions are available in supermarkets and specialty stores in most cities. And because Mexican cooking requires no special kitchen equipment, this book should find a welcome place in your home, useful both for family meals and entertaining.

When you experiment with Mexican cooking, we suggest that you do not limit yourself to preparing all-Mexican menus. One or two Mexican dishes introduced into a familiar meal will lend it lively interest. That is how American cuisine develops — in true "melting pot" tradition.

We hope that this book will inspire you to a fresh appreciation of the pleasures of Mexican cooking, of its healthful variety and of how easy it really is. We hope, too, that it will give you new standards for judging and demanding excellence and authenticity when you dine out in Mexican restaurants. And now, why not begin your Mexican cooking adventures with your very next meal?

¡Buen apetito!

The Betty Crocker Editors

Library of Congress Cataloging in Publication Data   Recipes by Romero, José Leopoldo, Betty Crocker's Mexican Cookbook.

Includes index.   1. Cookery, Mexican.   I. Crocker, Betty, pseud.   II. Title.   III. Title: Mexican Cookbook
TX716.M4R64   641.5972   80-6045   ISBN 0-394-51882-9

Manufactured in the United States of America   23456789   First Edition

# CONTENTS

# INTRODUCTION TO
# MEXICAN COOKING

The Mexican climate and growing conditions and the influences of history have made the cuisine of Mexico one of the most bountiful, colorful and richly varied in the world. Nearly every known fruit and vegetable is grown there, the unusually long coastline produces fish of many kinds and the turkey is native to Mexico.

All of this agricultural wealth is seen in the distinctive flavors of Mexican cooking. In the North of Mexico, chicken and tortillas, made of wheat rather than corn, are popular. As one travels south, pork, beef, corn and fruits become more prominent. But everywhere, beans are a mainstay of the national diet.

True Mexican cooking bears little resemblance to the restaurant fare familiar to us in the United States. It is neither oily and heavy nor highly seasoned. Chilies, while they are widely grown and used, are usually found only in sauces or used as a garnish or relish to be eaten at the discretion of the diner. Fresh vegetables are combined in leafy salads, and milk, although adults do not usually drink it, appears in the famous Mexican caramel custard called *flan* and in ice creams.

Mexican cooking had its beginnings in the cultures of the Aztec and Mayan Indians whose diets were based on corn and beans. In fact, corn was so revered that it was used in ceremonial worship of the Aztec goddess of fertility. As early as the 16th Century, ambassadors from Spain introduced cows and sheep, rice and spices to Mexico; and later, the French, Austrians and other Europeans visiting the New World left their imprint on its culture and its food supply. Today, the Mexican cuisine reflects all of these influences, contrasting simple and sophisticated dishes and blending the new with the old.

To understand Mexican cooking, it is helpful to know the daily eating patterns of the country. Mexicans eat on four or five separate occasions and often between meals. They are dedicated to snacking, and the variety of street food sold by vendors ranges from tacos and barbecued meat and fish snacks to sweet corn on sticks, fruit-flavored beverages and cakes, cookies and candy. The day begins with a light, early breakfast, *desayuno,* which usually means coffee and sweet rolls. By mid or late morning, it is time for a heartier breakfast, *almuerzo,* similar to our American brunch, with fruit, eggs, meat and dessert. *Comida* or dinner, the principal meal of the day, takes place in early afternoon and is traditionally followed by the siesta except when this interferes with modern business hours.

*Comida* can consist of as many as six courses, which would seem a great amount of food, except that serving portions are often small. It begins with an appetizer and continues with soup or a rice dish, followed by chicken or fish, a meat course, perhaps vegetables, and then salad and dessert. A light supper, called *merienda,* is eaten in the late afternoon or early evening. Like the English high tea, this is usually cake or cookies with Mexican *café con leche* rather than tea. Finally, the *cena,* a late evening supper, consists of a soup, stew or food left from an earlier meal and perhaps salad. Tortillas and beans accompany most of these meals, the beans usually served as a separate course.

To serve a Mexican meal attractively, no special accessories are necessary. However, Mexican cotton cloths, napkins, pottery, glass and tinware have a natural, casual beauty and colorful decoration which, while relatively inexpensive, contribute to the pleasures of dining in the Mexican manner.

*Clockwise from top: Tossed Romaine Salad, Tacos, Green beans, Chicken Cilantro, Mexican Rice, Guava Paste with Cream Cheese*

# SEASONINGS

The cooking of Mexico, like that of other countries, has distinctive herbs, spices and other seasonings typical of its authentic dishes. Those in Mexican food are quite common and readily available in most supermarkets or Mexican specialty food stores. Properly used, herbs and spices enhance the flavors of food rather than overpower them. It is recommended that you experiment with the amount of seasoning called for in each tested recipe in this book; then, determine by taste whether to increase or decrease the amount next time you prepare the recipe.

Dried herbs are more concentrated than fresh herbs. As a general rule, substitute ½ to 1 teaspoon dried herbs or ¼ teaspoon ground herbs for 1 tablespoon snipped fresh herbs.

Herbs and spices are perishable and should be stored tightly covered in a cool, dry place to prevent loss of flavor and caking of ground seasonings. Whole spices retain their flavor and aroma longer than when ground. It is practical to date new containers of both herbs and spices with a wax pencil or felt tip pen. Test for freshness and flavor at least once a year by rubbing a small amount on your fingertips and sniffing it. If there is no aroma, discard the container and replace it.

**1. Anise seed:** a small, oval seed that is usually greenish brown and identified with licorice flavor.

**2. Basil:** an herb which is a member of the mint family and turns a brownish olive green when dried. Sweet and warm in flavor with a pungent undertone.

**3. Camomile:** the dried white flower of the camomile plant, which resembles a tiny daisy, and is used for tea.

**4. Capers:** the pickled buds of the caper bush with a sharp flavor like that of a small gherkin.

**5. Chilies (Peppers)**

CHILIES, DRIED

   **a. Ancho:** probably the most commonly used chili in Mexico. It is the ripened, dried *poblano chile*. Wrinkled and deep reddish-brown, it turns brick red when softened in water.

   **b. Chipotle:** the ripened, dried and smoked *jalapeno chile*. Wrinkled and brown in color with a smoky odor.

CHILIES, FRESH

   **c. Jalapeno:** a small, hot chili, about 2½ inches long. Medium to dark green in color, with a smooth surface and rounded, tapered end. The seeds and veins vary from hot to very hot. Sold fresh and canned.

   **d. Poblano:** a dark green chili also called *ancho*

*or pasilla chile*. It varies from mild to medium hot and is ideal for stuffing.

    **e. Serrano:** a chili similar in appearance to the *jalapeno chile*, but smaller, slimmer and very hot. Sold canned and sometimes fresh.

CHILIES, CANNED

    **f. Green chilies:** usually *anaheim chiles* labeled as green chilies. They vary in degree of hotness depending on the number of seeds included when canned.

Note: wear rubber gloves when handling chilies to protect hands from irritation.

**6. Chili powder:** a blend of spices using chilies as the main ingredient. Other seasonings that can be added are cumin, oregano, garlic, onion, cloves and allspice. Chili powder varies in color from reddish to dark brown, depending on the chilies used.

**7. Cilantro** (Chinese parsley, Mexican parsley or fresh coriander): an herb with a willowy stem and broad, flat serrated leaf. Can be used as a garnish or a seasoning. Highly aromatic with a strong, distinctive flavor. No known substitute.

**8. Cinnamon:** a pungent, sweet spice that comes from the dried bark of trees in the evergreen family. Sold as sticks or ground.

**9. Coriander:** a dried, ripe berry which is a member of the parsley family. The small seed ranges in color from white to yellow, with a mild, distinctive

taste like a combination of lemon peel and sage. Sold whole or ground.

**10. Cumin:** the predominant flavor in chili powder with a strong, dry taste similar to caraway. Sold both whole and ground.

**11. Nutmeg:** an oval brown seed of the peach-like fruit of a tropical evergreen tree. The ground spice has a sweet flavor with a warm, spicy undertone. Sold whole and ground.

**12. Oregano:** a strong and aromatic herb with an assertive, pleasantly bitter undertone. Sold dried and ground.

**13. Saffron:** very expensive because the dried stigmas of the crocus plant must be hand picked. Pleasantly bitter in flavor and known for the yellow color it gives food.

**14. Sage:** an herb with a strong, aromatic odor and a somewhat astringent and bitter flavor. Sold whole, rubbed or ground. (The rubbed and ground sage are very similar because the high oil content of the leaves prevents the ground sage from becoming compact.)

**15. Tarragon:** an herb with piquant flavor reminiscent of anise. Sold dried or ground.

**16. Thyme:** a member of the mint family. When dried, leaves turn a dull, grey green. "Dry" aromatic and pungent flavor. Sold dried or ground.

# INGREDIENTS

**1. Avocado:** pear-shaped or oval fruit with an outside shell that varies in color from shades of green to purplish-black. The ripened fruit inside has a rich flavor and soft, oily texture.

**2. Beans:**
  **a. Black -** small, black beans, sometimes called turtle beans, with hearty, distinctive flavor. Sold dried or canned.
  **b. Garbanzo -** or chick-pea is a widely cultivated round beige colored legume with a nut-like flavor. Sold dried or canned.
  **c. Pinto -** small, beige colored beans with brown specks, which received their name from the Spanish word *pinto* meaning "paint." Sold dried or canned.

**3. Bell Peppers:** the green and red bell peppers, familiar in the United States, and used in Mexican cooking. Green peppers turn red in the fall, becoming sweeter and milder yet retaining their crisp, firm texture.

**4. Cactus (nopalitos):** the young, pad-like growth of some varieties of edible cacti with texture and flavor like green beans. Sometimes sold in the United States as "prickly pear."

**5. Chayote:** a pear-shaped squash with a smooth or ribbed outside and a light green or creamy white inside. Similar in flavor and appearance to a bland honeydew melon. Should be firm and unwrinkled.

**6. Cheese:** since good Mexican cheese is rarely found in the United States, we have substituted readily available cheese such as (a) Monterey Jack, (b) Cheddar and (c) Parmesan which are similar to the Mexican *queso.*

**7. Chorizo:** a highly spiced Mexican sausage made from pork, beef or a combination of the two. Similar to Italian sausages in flavor and spiciness.

**8. Corn Husks:** the dried shucks of corn traditionally used as wrapping for tamales. Sold in Mexican specialty food stores. Ready to use after being softened in warm water for several hours. Small husks must be overlapped to make one large enough to hold tamale filling.

**9. Guava Paste:** a paste made from the pulp of the guava fruit, which has been cooked with sugar until very thick. It is formed into a block or round and sold canned.

**10. Hominy:** a starchy vegetable prepared from the mature kernels of regular field corn. The corn kernels are soaked, cooked slightly and the hard outer covering removed.

**11. Jicama:** a crisp, sweet white root vegetable served cooked as well as eaten raw. Shaped like a turnip, with a thin brown skin and varying in size.

**12. Mangos:** plump, juicy, deep gold tropical fruit with reddish yellow skin. Varies in shape from round to oval.

**13. Masa Harina:** instant corn flour used in Mexican cooking. Made by soaking and boiling corn kernels in lime water and then grinding into a very fine powder. Sold in the specialty food sections of some supermarkets or at a Mexican specialty food store.

**14. Plantain:** a firm, starchy vegetable that resembles a large banana and is served cooked. The thick outer peel must be removed before using.

**15. Pumpkin Seeds:** the hulled, unsalted seed of the pumpkin. Should be stored in a cool, dry place to prevent rancidity. Sold in health food stores or specialty food stores.

**16. Tamarind:** the fruit of the tamarind tree which has flat pods containing several seeds and a brown pulp. Acid in flavor and is used with sugar to make a refreshing beverage. Sold in the pods or cleaned.

**17. Tomatillos:** small green tomatoes with thin, paper-like covering They turn from green to yellow as they ripen but generally are used while still in the green state. Sold fresh and canned.

**18. Tortilla:** flat bread made from (a) corn or (b) wheat flour and considered the national bread of Mexico. It is the basic ingredient of such foods as tacos, enchiladas, burritos and quesadillas.

# MENUS

Experimenting with the recipes in this book will be enjoyable and satisfying. You will find that a Mexican main dish served with a vegetable or a salad, tortillas, beans, and fresh fruit in place of dessert, compose a substantial meal. As your confidence grows, you will progress to full-course Mexican menus not only for your family but also for entertaining. The menus that follow illustrate the range of colors, flavors and textures of Mexican dishes and suggest combinations to guide you in planning your own menus.

## SUMMER LUNCHEON

Avocado Soup

Corn Soufflé

Wilted Spinach

Mango-Honey Ice Cream

## EASY MEXICAN PARTY

Avocado Dip

Garlic Soup

Beef Burritos

Mexican Rice

Fruit Compote

## MEXICAN DINNER

Hot Broth

Cod with Garlic

Mexican Rice

Vegetable Pears

Spinach and Mushroom Salad

Crepes with Caramel Filling

Mexican Coffee

## MEXICAN BUFFET

Avocado Dip

Meatballs in Chile Sauce

Cold Meat and Vegetables

Green Enchiladas

Broiled Bean Sandwiches

Festive Tricolor Salad

Hot Pickled Vegetables

Mango Mousse

## MEXICAN COCKTAIL PARTY

Corn and Walnut Dip

Pinto Bean Dip

Cucumber Wedges

Chips with Cheese

Fried Rolled Tacos

Chartreuse Cocktails

## WINTER NIGHT SUPPER

Beer and Cheese Soup

Egg and Potato Scramble

Zucchini with Lime and Cilantro

Fried Sweet Puffs

Flaming Coffee

## DINNER FOR FOUR

Chicken Almendrado

Refried Beans

Sautéed Mushrooms

Cauliflower with Cheese Sauce

Oranges and Cinnamon

## DINNER FOR COMPANY

Peppers Stuffed with Tuna

Mexican Pot Roast

Eggplant Fritters

Mexican Succotash

Orange Salad with Pecan Dressing

Cognac Custard

## QUICK DINNER

Chicken Cilantro

Mexican Rice

Green Beans

Tossed Romaine Salad

Tortillas

Guava Paste with Cream Cheese

## FESTIVE DINNER

Stuffed Oysters

Stuffed Flank Steak

Mexican Rice

Carrots with Green Grapes

Cactus Salad

Sautéed Strawberries

## MEXICAN BRUNCH

Tortilla Skillet

Eggs with Sardines

Baked Stuffed Tomatoes

Pears Stuffed with Dates

Mexican Coffee

# Appetizers

## Chips with Cheese
### (Nachos)

6  Flour or Corn Tortillas (page 32)
1½  cups shredded cheese (about 6 ounces)
6  jalapeno peppers

Heat oil (1 inch) to 365°. Fry tortillas 1 at a time, holding tortilla down in oil with tongs, until light brown, about 1 minute. Drain on paper towels.

Place tortillas on ungreased cookie sheet. Sprinkle ¼ cup cheese evenly over each tortilla. Seed and cut each jalapeno pepper into 6 strips; arrange strips on top of cheese. Set oven control to broil and/or 550°. Broil tortillas with tops 3 to 4 inches from heat until cheese is melted. Cut each tortilla into 6 wedges. *3 dozen appetizers.*

## Plantain Chips
### (Plátanos Fritos)

Vegetable oil
4  plantains, cut into ¼-inch slices
1  tablespoon chili powder
½  teaspoon salt

Heat oil (1 inch) to 350°. Fry plantains in hot oil until golden brown, about 2 minutes. Drain on paper towels; toss with chili powder and salt. *About 5 cups chips.*

## Jicama Appetizer
### (Jicama con Limón y Chile)

1  jicama (about 2 pounds)
   Juice of 1 lemon (about ¼ cup)
1  teaspoon salt
1  teaspoon chili powder

Peel jicama; cut into fourths. Cut each fourth into ¼-inch slices. Arrange slices on serving plate. Drizzle with lemon juice; sprinkle with salt and chili powder. Refrigerate until chilled, at least 2 hours. *About 3½ dozen appetizers.*

## Cucumber Wedges
### (Pepinos)

2  medium cucumbers
1  tablespoon lime juice
1  teaspoon coarse salt
½  teaspoon chili powder

Cut cucumbers lengthwise into fourths; cut fourths into 2-inch pieces. Place cucumbers in single layer on serving plate. Drizzle with lime juice; sprinkle with salt and chili powder. *About 2½ dozen appetizers.*

*Top left: Cucumber Wedges; Center: Jicama Appetizer;*
*Top right: Plantain Chips; Bottom: Chips with Cheese*

*Fried Rolled Tacos*

# Fried Rolled Tacos
## (Flautas)

    Avocado Dip (page 17)
1   cup finely chopped cooked chicken
12  Flour Tortillas (page 32)
    Vegetable oil

Prepare Avocado Dip; cover and refrigerate. Spoon 1 tablespoon chicken across bottom of each tortilla. Roll up tightly; secure with wooden picks.

Heat oil (1 inch) to 350°. Fry flautas, turning once, until golden brown, about 2 minutes. Drain on paper towels; remove wooden picks. Serve with Avocado Dip. *1 dozen appetizers.*

# Peanuts in Chile
## (Cacahuates con Chile)

2   cloves garlic, crushed
1   teaspoon vegetable oil
1   cup shelled raw peanuts
1   tablespoon chili powder
1/2 teaspoon salt

Cook and stir garlic in oil in 8-inch skillet over medium heat until golden brown; remove garlic. Add peanuts and chili powder. Cook and stir until peanuts are warm, about 2 minutes. Drain on paper towels; sprinkle with salt. *1 cup peanuts.*

# Corn and Onion Fritters
## (Frituras de Elote con Cebolla)

1  cup chopped onion
2  tablespoons margarine or butter
1  can (16½ ounces) whole kernel corn, drained
1  jar (4 ounces) chopped pimiento, drained
¾  teaspoon salt
¼  teaspoon pepper
   Vegetable oil
1  cup all-purpose flour
½  cup shredded cheese (about 2 ounces)
1  teaspoon baking powder
½  cup milk
2  eggs, separated

Cook and stir onion in margarine until tender. Stir in corn, pimiento, salt and pepper; cool.

Heat oil (1 inch) to 375°. Mix corn mixture, flour, cheese and baking powder. Stir in milk and egg yolks. Beat egg whites in small mixer bowl until stiff but not dry. Fold corn mixture into egg whites.

Drop batter by rounded teaspoonfuls into hot oil. Fry until golden brown, turning once, about 1 minute. Drain on paper towels. *About 4 dozen appetizers.*

# Ham and Cheese Appetizer
## (Sincronizadas de Jamón y Queso)

6  thin slices fully cooked smoked ham
6  Flour Tortillas (page 32)
3  slices Muenster or mild Cheddar cheese
6  tablespoons vegetable oil

Place 1 slice ham on each of 3 tortillas. Add cheese. Top with remaining slice ham; cover with remaining tortilla.

Heat 2 tablespoons of the oil in 6-inch skillet over medium heat until hot. Fry 1 sandwich, turning once, until golden brown and cheese is melted, about 3 minutes. Cut into 4 wedges. Repeat with remaining sandwiches. *1 dozen appetizers.*

# Mexican Deviled Eggs
## (Huevos Endiablados)

12  hard-cooked eggs
¼   cup mayonnaise or salad dressing
1   jalapeno pepper, seeded and finely chopped
1   tablespoon ground cumin
1   tablespoon finely chopped capers
1   tablespoon prepared mustard
½   teaspoon salt
    Chili powder
    Finely snipped cilantro

Cut peeled eggs lengthwise into halves. Slip out yolks; mash with fork. Stir in mayonnaise, pepper, cumin, capers, mustard and salt; mix until smooth.

Fill egg whites with egg yolk mixture, heaping lightly. Sprinkle with chili powder; garnish with cilantro. *2 dozen appetizers.*

# Meatballs in Chile Sauce
## (Albóndigas en Salsa de Chile)

3   Corn Tortillas (page 32), cut into small pieces
½   cup milk
½   pound ground beef
½   pound ground pork
½   pound finely chopped fully cooked smoked ham
1   small onion, chopped (about ¼ cup)
1   clove garlic, finely chopped
1   teaspoon ground cumin
1   teaspoon dried oregano leaves
½   teaspoon salt
¼   teaspoon pepper
1   cup Basic Red Sauce (page 65)
1   cup Beef Broth (page 26)

Soak tortillas in milk in large bowl 15 minutes. Add remaining ingredients except Basic Red Sauce and Beef Broth; mix completely. Shape mixture into 1-inch balls. Heat red sauce and beef broth to boiling in 10-inch skillet; reduce heat. Add meatballs. Cover and simmer until done, 15 to 20 minutes. *About 3½ dozen meatballs.*

# Stuffed Mushrooms
## (Hongos Rellenos)

24  medium mushrooms
 2  tablespoons margarine or butter
¼  cup chopped onion
 2  tablespoons dry white wine
¼  cup dry bread crumbs
¼  cup finely chopped fully cooked smoked ham
 2  tablespoons snipped parsley
 1  tablespoon lime juice
 1  clove garlic, finely chopped
 1  teaspoon dried oregano leaves
    Dash of pepper
½  cup finely shredded cheese (about 2 ounces)

Cut stems from mushrooms; finely chop enough stems to measure ¼ cup. Heat margarine in 10-inch skillet until margarine begins to bubble. Cook mushroom caps top sides down until light brown; remove caps with slotted spoon.

Cook and stir onion in same skillet until tender. Stir in wine. Simmer uncovered 2 minutes. Stir in chopped mushroom stems and remaining ingredients except cheese; mix completely. Cool slightly.

Shape stuffing into 24 small balls; place 1 in each mushroom cap. Sprinkle with cheese. Set oven control to broil and/or 550°. Broil with tops 3 to 4 inches from heat until cheese is melted, about 3 minutes. *2 dozen appetizers.*

# Stuffed Oysters
## (Ostiones Rellenos)

12  oysters in shells
½  cup clam juice
½  cup white wine
    Juice of 1 lime
¼  cup margarine or butter
 1  cup dry bread crumbs
½  cup toasted sesame seed
¼  cup Herbed Vinaigrette (page 21)
¼  cup Casera Sauce (page 65)
¼  cup snipped parsley
 1  tablespoon finely chopped fully cooked
       smoked ham
 1  cup shredded cheese (about 4 ounces)

Remove oysters from shells; reserve 12 half shells. Heat clam juice, wine and lime juice to boiling; reduce heat. Simmer uncovered until reduced to 1 cup. Add margarine and oysters. Simmer oysters in clam juice mixture 2 minutes; do not overcook. Remove oysters with slotted spoon; keep warm.

Stir remaining ingredients except cheese into clam juice mixture; mix completely. Divide half the stuffing among shells. Top each with oyster. Cover each with remaining stuffing; sprinkle with cheese. Set oven control to broil and/or 550°. Broil 2 to 3 inches from heat until cheese is melted, 3 to 4 minutes. *1 dozen appetizers.*

## *How to Make Tortilla Chips*

*1. Cut flour or corn tortillas into wedges with a kitchen scissor.*

*2. Heat vegetable oil (1 inch) to 365°. Fry wedges until crisp and golden brown, about 1 minute.*

*3. Drain on paper towels. Sprinkle with salt if desired.*

# Corn and Walnut Dip
## (Salsa de Elote con Nueces)

2   *packages (8 ounces each) cream cheese, softened*
1/4  *cup vegetable oil*
    *Juice of 1 lime (about 1/4 cup)*
1   *tablespoon chili powder*
1   *tablespoon ground cumin*
1/2  *teaspoon salt*
    *Dash of pepper*
1   *can (8 3/4 ounces) whole kernel corn, drained*
1   *cup chopped walnuts*
1   *small onion, chopped (about 1/4 cup)*

Beat cream cheese, oil, lime juice, chili powder, cumin, salt and pepper in bowl on medium speed until smooth. Stir in corn, walnuts and onion. Serve with tortilla chips if desired. *4 cups dip.*

# Pinto Bean Dip
## (Salsa de Puré de Frijol)

2   *cups cooked Pinto Beans (page 79)*
1/2  *cup Casera Sauce (page 65)*
1/2  *cup Herbed Vinaigrette (page 21)*
1   *tablespoon finely chopped fully cooked smoked ham*
1   *teaspoon salt*
1/2  *teaspoon ground cumin*
    *Dash of pepper*

Place all ingredients in blender container. Cover and blend on medium speed until smooth. Serve with tortilla chips if desired. *About 2 cups dip.*

# Bean and Garlic Dip
## (Salsa de Puré de Frijol con Ajo)

2   *cups Pinto Beans (page 79)*
1/4  *cup mayonnaise or salad dressing*
1   *clove garlic, finely chopped*
1 1/2  *teaspoons chili powder*
1/4  *teaspoon salt*
    *Dash of pepper*

Mix all ingredients. Cover and refrigerate 1 hour. Serve with tortilla chips if desired. *About 2 cups dip.*

*Avocado Dip*

# Avocado Dip
## (Guacamole)

2   *large ripe avocados, mashed*
2   *tomatoes, finely chopped*
1   *medium onion, chopped (about 1/2 cup)*
2   *jalapeno peppers, seeded and finely chopped*
1   *clove garlic, finely chopped*
2   *tablespoons finely snipped cilantro*
1   *tablespoon vegetable oil*
    *Juice of 1/2 lime (about 2 tablespoons)*
1/2  *teaspoon salt*
    *Dash of pepper*

Mix all ingredients in glass or plastic bowl. Cover and refrigerate at least 1 hour. Serve with tortilla chips. *2 1/2 cups dip.*

# Avocado and Raisin Dip
## (Salsa de Aguacate con Pasas)

2   avocados, cut up
1/2   cup raisins
1/2   cup vegetable oil
      Juice of 1 lime (about 1/4 cup)
1   teaspoon sugar
1   teaspoon salt
1/4   teaspoon freshly ground pepper

Place all ingredients in blender container. Cover and blend on high speed until smooth, about 45 seconds. Serve with raw vegetables, assorted crackers or fried tortillas. *1²/₃ cups dip.*

# Baked Cheese
## (Queso Asado)

1   cup shredded Cheddar cheese (about 4 ounces)
1   cup shredded Muenster cheese (about 4 ounces)
1   cup shredded mozzarella cheese (about 4 ounces)
1   Spiced Sausage (page 51), cooked and
      cut into 6 slices

Mix cheeses; divide mixture among 6 ungreased 6-ounce custard cups. Top each with sausage. Place cups on cookie sheet. Cook uncovered in 350° oven until cheese is melted, about 15 minutes. Serve with tortilla chips if desired. *6 servings.*

# Chilies with Cheese
## (Chile con Queso)

1   cup shredded Cheddar or Monterey Jack cheese
      (about 4 ounces)
1   can (4 ounces) chopped green chilies, drained
1/4   cup half-and-half
2   tablespoons finely chopped onion
2   teaspoons ground cumin
1/2   teaspoon salt

Heat all ingredients over low heat, stirring constantly, until cheese is melted. Serve with tortilla chips if desired. *1¹/₄ cups dip.*

# Cold Meat and Vegetables
## (Fiambre)

12   to 15 thin slices Genoa salami
12   to 15 thin slices cooked roast beef
3   Spiced Sausages (page 51), cooked and sliced
1   can (6¹/₂ ounces) tuna, drained
1   can (1³/₄ ounces) rolled anchovy fillets
3   hard-cooked eggs, cut into fourths
12   to 15 stalks cooked asparagus
6   to 8 cooked artichoke hearts, cut into halves
3   tomatoes, cut into wedges
1   cup sliced cooked potatoes
1   cup sliced cooked beets
1   cup cooked green beans
1   cup cooked garbanzo beans
      Lettuce leaves
1¹/₂   cups Herbed Vinaigrette (double recipe, page 21)
1/4   cup capers
1   small red onion, thinly sliced

Arrange meats, fish, eggs and vegetables in separate sections on lettuce. Pour on Herbed Vinaigrette; garnish with capers and onion. Cover and refrigerate at least 1 hour. *12 to 15 servings.*

# Crab and Avocado Cocktail
## (Coctel de Jaiba con Aguacate)

1   cup cooked crabmeat
2   avocados, cut up
2   jalapeno peppers, seeded and finely chopped
1/4   cup chopped tomato
      Juice of 1 lime (about 1/4 cup)
2   tablespoons olive or vegetable oil
2   tablespoons chopped onion
2   tablespoons snipped cilantro
1   clove garlic, finely chopped
3/4   teaspoon salt
      Dash of pepper
1¹/₂   cups finely shredded lettuce
      Lime or lemon wedges

Mix all ingredients except lettuce and lime. Place 1/4 cup lettuce in each of 6 serving dishes. Divide crabmeat mixture among dishes. Garnish with lime. *6 servings.*

# Stuffed Avocado and Crab
## (Aguacate Relleno con Jaiba)

3    ripe avocados
1    cup cooked crabmeat
¼    cup snipped cilantro
1    small onion, chopped (about ¼ cup)
¼    cup finely chopped celery
¼    cup finely chopped carrots
¼    cup Herbed Vinaigrette (page 21)
½    cup mayonnaise or salad dressing
1    teaspoon ground cumin
½    teaspoon salt
     Dash of pepper
6    radish roses

Cut 2 of the avocados lengthwise into halves; re-move pits. Carefully scoop out pulp, leaving peels intact and reserve. Mash pulp. Cut remaining avo-cado lengthwise into halves. Remove pit. Carefully remove pulp leaving both pulp and peel intact; reserve peels. Cut avocado pulp into 12 slices.

Mix mashed avocado and remaining ingredients except avocado slices and radishes. Divide mixture among avocado peels. Garnish with radishes and avocado slices. *6 servings.*

## ABOUT AVOCADOS

The favorite fruit of Mexico is the avocado which grows in many regions. The avocado is eaten as a salad, in sauces, eaten plain with salt and lime or in cooked dishes such as soups and stews.

Ripened avocados have a rich, nut-like oily flavor. A ripe avocado is soft and yields to gentle pressure. A hard avocado will ripen in several days at room temperature.

To make avocado shells, cut avocado in half lengthwise, twisting gently to separate the halves. Strike a knife directly into the seed and twist to lift it out. Peel avocado halves and place cut side down to prevent breaking when cutting them into slices.

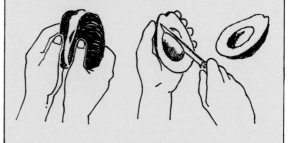

## Peppers Stuffed with Tuna
### (Chiles con Atún)

*Herbed Vinaigrette (below)*
1    *can (6½ ounces) tuna, drained*
2    *tablespoons finely chopped onion*
2    *tablespoons finely chopped carrot*
2    *tablespoons finely chopped celery*
2    *tablespoons snipped parsley*
¼    *cup mayonnaise or salad dressing*
8    *poblano peppers*
1    *medium onion, thinly sliced*
2    *tablespoons capers*

Prepare Herbed Vinaigrette. Mix tuna, 2 tablespoons onion, carrot, celery, parsley and mayonnaise. Slit peppers lengthwise down one side; remove stems, seeds and membranes. Stuff each pepper with tuna mixture. Place peppers cut sides down in serving dish. Pour vinaigrette over peppers; garnish with onion and capers. Cover and refrigerate until chilled. *8 appetizers.*

### Herbed Vinaigrette

½    *cup olive or vegetable oil*
1    *tablespoon wine vinegar*
      *Juice of ½ lemon (about 2 tablespoons)*
      *Juice of ½ lime (about 2 tablespoons)*
1    *clove garlic, finely chopped*
½    *teaspoon dry mustard*
¼    *teaspoon dried oregano leaves*
¼    *teaspoon dried basil leaves*
1    *teaspoon snipped parsley*
¼    *teaspoon ground sage*
¼    *teaspoon salt*
⅛    *teaspoon freshly ground pepper*

Shake all ingredients in tightly covered jar. *¾ cup.*

## Mexican Style Shrimp Cocktail
### (Coctel de Camarón)

24    *fresh or frozen raw medium shrimp*
1    *cup water*
      *Juice of 2 limes*
1    *clove garlic, finely chopped*
2    *teaspoons salt*
      *Dash of pepper*
¼    *cup chopped tomato*
1    *small avocado, chopped*
2    *jalapeno peppers, seeded and finely chopped*
2    *tablespoons chopped onion*
2    *tablespoons finely chopped carrot*
2    *tablespoons snipped cilantro*
2    *tablespoons olive or vegetable oil*
1½    *cups finely shredded lettuce*
      *Lemon or lime wedges*

Peel shrimp. (If shrimp is frozen, do not thaw; peel under running cold water.) Make a shallow cut lengthwise down back of each shrimp; wash out sand vein.

Heat water, lime juice, garlic, salt and pepper to boiling in 4-quart Dutch oven; reduce heat. Simmer uncovered until reduced to ⅔ cup. Add shrimp. Cover and simmer 3 minutes; do not overcook. Immediately remove shrimp from liquid with slotted spoon and place in bowl of iced water. Simmer liquid until reduced to 2 tablespoons; cool and reserve.

Mix liquid, shrimp and remaining ingredients except lettuce and lemon in glass or plastic bowl. Cover and refrigerate at least 1 hour. Just before serving, place ¼ cup lettuce on each of 6 serving dishes. Divide shrimp mixture among dishes. Garnish with lemon. *6 servings.*

# Soups

## Zucchini Soup
### (Sopa Xochitl)

1   small onion, chopped (about ¼ cup)
1   tablespoon margarine or butter
2   cups Chicken Broth (page 26)
2   small zucchini, chopped
1   can (8¾ ounces) whole kernel corn, drained*
2   tablespoons finely chopped canned roasted
         green chilies
½   teaspoon salt
⅛   teaspoon pepper
1   cup milk
2   ounces Monterey Jack cheese, cut into ¼-inch
         cubes (about ½ cup)
     Ground nutmeg
     Snipped parsley

Cook and stir onion in margarine in 2-quart sauce-pan until tender. Stir in Chicken Broth, zucchini, corn, green chilies, salt and pepper. Heat to boiling; reduce heat. Cover and cook until zucchini is tender, about 5 minutes. Stir in milk; heat until hot. Add cheese; garnish with nutmeg and parsley. *5 or 6 servings (about 1 cup each).*

*1 package (10 ounces) frozen whole kernel corn can be substituted for the canned corn.

## Beer and Cheese Soup
### (Sopa de Cerveza y Queso)

1   medium onion, chopped (about ½ cup)
2   tablespoons margarine or butter
1   bottle (12 ounces) beer
½   cup finely chopped carrots
½   cup finely chopped celery
2   cups Chicken Broth (page 26)
1   teaspoon salt
1   teaspoon ground cumin
¼   teaspoon ground nutmeg
     Dash of ground cloves
     Dash of pepper
1   cup dairy sour cream
4   ounces Cheddar or Monterey Jack cheese,
         cut into ¼-inch cubes (about 1 cup)

Cook and stir onion in margarine in 2-quart sauce-pan until tender. Stir in beer, carrots and celery. Heat to boiling; reduce heat. Cover and simmer 10 minutes.

Stir in Chicken Broth, salt, cumin, nutmeg, cloves and pepper. Heat to boiling; reduce heat. Cover and simmer 30 minutes. Remove from heat; stir in sour cream. Sprinkle with cheese. *5 servings (about 1 cup each).*

*Zucchini Soup*

# Vegetable Chicken Soup
## (Sopa de Pollo con Vegetales)

1   chipotle pepper
¼   cup vegetable oil
4   tortillas, cut into ¼-inch strips
½   cup chopped onion
1   cup chopped carrots
1   cup chopped celery
4   cups Chicken Broth (page 26)
½   cup chopped chicken
¼   cup orange juice
2   tablespoons lime juice
1   tablespoon lemon juice
    Dairy sour cream

Cover chipotle pepper with boiling water. Let stand until soft, about 30 minutes; drain. Remove stem and seeds. Chop pepper finely.

Heat oil in 3-quart saucepan until hot. Fry tortilla strips, stirring occasionally, until crisp and golden brown. Remove and drain on paper towels.

Cook and stir onion in same saucepan until tender. Stir in remaining ingredients except sour cream. Heat to boiling; reduce heat. Cover and simmer 20 minutes. Garnish with tortilla strips and sour cream. *6 servings (about ¾ cup each).*

# Tripe Stew
## (Menudo)

2   pounds honeycomb tripe
4   whole cloves
1   medium onion, cut into fourths
3   cups Chicken Broth (page 26)
2   cups water
½   cup chopped carrots
½   cup chopped celery
1   can (16 ounces) whole tomatoes
3   cloves garlic, finely chopped
1   teaspoon salt
½   teaspoon ground oregano
½   teaspoon ground sage
½   teaspoon pepper
1   tablespoon olive or vegetable oil

Rinse tripe under cold water. Place tripe and enough water to cover in bowl. Let stand 2 hours; drain. Repeat. Cut tripe into strips, 2 × ¼ inches.

Insert 1 clove into each onion fourth. Heat tripe, onions and remaining ingredients except oil to boiling; reduce heat. Cover and simmer until tripe is tender, about 4 hours. Stir in oil. Sprinkle with finely chopped scallions and snipped cilantro if desired. *8 servings (about 1 cup each).*

# Bean Soup
## (Sopa de Frijol)

4   cups bean broth (page 79)
1   cup cooked pinto or black beans
½   cup shredded Muenster or Cheddar cheese
        (about 2 ounces)
½   cup Casera Sauce (page 65)
⅔   cup shredded Muenster or Cheddar cheese
        (about 3 ounces)
    Chopped cilantro

Place 1 cup of the bean broth, the beans, ½ cup cheese and the Casera Sauce in blender container. Cover and blend on high speed until smooth. Heat broth mixture and remaining broth to boiling; reduce heat. Cover and simmer 10 minutes. Sprinkle each serving with 2 tablespoons cheese and the cilantro. *5 servings (1 cup each).*

## ABOUT BEANS

Beans are an accompaniment to every meal, including breakfast, in many Mexican homes. Usually prepared in large quantities, beans are served the first day with their broth, often with an onion and cilantro garnish. As beans are reheated, the broth thickens and the beans develop a paste-like texture. They are then mashed and fried in lard or oil and become the famous Mexican "refried" beans.

All dried beans are high in vegetable protein, which is fortified when combined with that in meats and dairy products. Store dried beans tightly covered in a dry place 6 to 8 months.

# Pork and Hominy Soup
## (Pozole)

1/4   cup vegetable oil
1    clove garlic
1/2   pound pork boneless shoulder, cut
          into 1/2-inch cubes
1/4   cup all-purpose flour
1    medium onion, chopped (about 1/2 cup)
2    cups cooked Pinto Beans (page 79)
1    can (30 ounces) hominy, drained
1/4   cup chopped carrot
1/4   cup chopped celery
1/4   cup chopped green chilies
1    tablespoon chili powder
3    cups Chicken Broth (page 26)
1    teaspoon salt
1/4   teaspoon pepper
1 1/2  teaspoons dried oregano leaves
1    small onion, chopped (about 1/4 cup)
1/4   cup snipped cilantro

Heat 1/4 cup oil and the garlic in 3-quart saucepan until hot. Coat pork with flour. Cook and stir pork over medium heat until brown; remove from saucepan. Cook and stir 1/2 cup onion in same saucepan until tender. Stir in Pinto Beans, hominy, carrot, celery, green chilies and chili powder. Heat to boiling; reduce heat. Cover and simmer 10 minutes.

Stir pork, Chicken Broth, salt and pepper into vegetable mixture. Heat to boiling; reduce heat. Cover and simmer 30 minutes. Sprinkle with oregano, 1/4 cup chopped onion and the cilantro. *6 servings (about 1 cup each).*

# Spinach and Potato Soup
## (Sopa de Papa y Espinaca)

2    slices bacon, cut up
1    medium onion, chopped (about 1/2 cup)
2    cups Chicken Broth (page 26)
2    cups diced potatoes
1/4   cup finely chopped carrot
1/4   cup finely chopped celery
1/4   cup dry white wine
1    teaspoon salt
1/2   teaspoon dried thyme leaves
1/2   teaspoon dried sage leaves
1/2   teaspoon pepper
2    pounds spinach, chopped
2    cups milk
1/2   cup snipped parsley
1    Spiced Sausage (page 51), cooked and
          cut into 6 slices

Cook and stir bacon in 3-quart saucepan until crisp; remove bacon and drain on paper towel. Cook and stir onion in same saucepan until tender. Stir in Chicken Broth, potatoes, carrot, celery, wine, salt, thyme, sage and pepper. Heat to boiling; reduce heat. Cover and simmer 30 minutes.

Add half the spinach; cover and cook 2 minutes. Add remaining spinach; cover and cook just until spinach is wilted, about 2 minutes. Stir in milk, parsley and bacon; heat just until hot. Garnish with sausage. *6 servings (about 1 cup each).*

# Shrimp Soup
## (Sopa de Camarón)

*½    pound small fresh or frozen raw shrimp*
*4    cups Chicken Broth (below)*
*¼    cup Casera Sauce (page 65)*
*½    teaspoon salt*
*⅛    teaspoon ground saffron*
*     Dash of pepper*
*1    teaspoon cornstarch*
*1    tablespoon cold water*
*½    cup half-and-half*
*¼    cup snipped parsley*

Peel shrimp. (If shrimp is frozen, do not thaw; peel under running cold water.) Make a shallow cut lengthwise down back of each shrimp; wash out sand vein. Chop shrimp. Place shrimp, 1 cup of the Chicken Broth and the Casera Sauce in blender container. Cover and blend on high speed until smooth. Heat shrimp mixture, the remaining broth, salt, saffron and pepper to boiling.

Mix cornstarch and water; stir into shrimp mixture. Heat to boiling; cook and stir 1 minute. Remove from heat; stir in half-and-half. Sprinkle with parsley. *5 servings (about 1 cup each).*

# Chicken Broth
## (Caldo de Pollo)

*4    to 5-pound stewing chicken, cut up*
*2    medium tomatoes, cut into fourths*
*1    large stalk celery (with leaves), cut into pieces*
*1    medium carrot, cut into pieces*
*1    medium onion, cut into fourths*
*3    cloves garlic*
*2    teaspoons salt*
*½    teaspoon dried sage leaves*
*½    teaspoon dried thyme leaves*
*½    teaspoon pepper*

Remove any excess pieces of fat from chicken. Place chicken, giblets and neck in 4-quart Dutch oven. Add just enough water to cover. Add remaining ingredients. Heat to boiling; reduce heat. Cover and simmer until thickest pieces are tender, about 45 minutes. Refrigerate chicken in broth until cool.

When cool, remove chicken from bones and skin in large pieces. Skim fat from broth; strain. Cover and refrigerate chicken pieces and broth separately no longer than 24 hours. Use in any recipe calling for cooked chicken or chicken broth. *About 4 cups cut-up cooked chicken and 7 cups broth.*

*Note:* Reconstituted canned chicken broth can be substituted in recipes calling for Chicken Broth.

# Beef Broth
## (Caldo de Carne de Res)

*4    whole cloves*
*1    medium onion, cut into fourths*
*2    pounds beef boneless chuck, tip or round,
      cut into 1½-inch cubes*
*2    stalks celery (with leaves), cut into pieces*
*2    cloves garlic, crushed*
*1    green pepper, cut into pieces*
*1    bay leaf*
*1    tablespoon dried oregano leaves*
*1    teaspoon salt*
*½    teaspoon pepper*

Insert 1 clove into each onion piece. Place onion and remaining ingredients in 4-quart Dutch oven. Add just enough water to cover. Heat to boiling; reduce heat. Cover and simmer until beef is tender, 2½ to 3 hours. Remove beef from broth. Skim fat from broth; strain. Cover and refrigerate beef and broth separately no longer than 24 hours. Beef can be shredded and used in recipes calling for cooked beef. *About 3 cups cooked beef and 5 cups broth.*

*Note:* Reconstituted canned beef broth or consommé can be substituted in recipes calling for Beef Broth.

*It is easy to shred warm, cooked meat with two forks.*

# Avocado Soup
## (Sopa de Aguacate)

3 cups Chicken Broth (page 26)
1 cup half-and-half
2 large avocados, cut up
1 clove garlic, crushed
1 tablespoon chopped onion
¾ teaspoon salt
¼ teaspoon snipped cilantro
  Dash of pepper

Place 1½ cups of the Chicken Broth and the remaining ingredients in blender container. Cover and blend on medium speed until smooth. Stir remaining broth into avocado mixture. Cover and refrigerate until chilled, about 2 hours. Garnish with sour cream and paprika or avocado slices if desired. *6 servings (about ¾ cup each).*

# Tortilla Dumpling Soup
## (Sopa de Albóndiga de Tortilla)

4 cups Chicken Broth (page 26)
¼ cup Casera Sauce (page 65)
½ cup masa harina
½ teaspoon baking powder
½ teaspoon chili powder
¼ teaspoon salt
2 tablespoons chopped onion
1 tablespoon snipped parsley
1 egg
2 tablespoons milk

Heat Chicken Broth and Casera Sauce to boiling. Mix masa harina, baking powder, chili powder, salt, onion, parsley and egg. Stir in milk. Shape dough by teaspoonfuls into small balls; add to broth mixture. Cover and cook 15 minutes. Sprinkle with chopped green onion if desired. *8 servings (½ cup each).*

*Avocado Soup and Tortilla Dumpling Soup*

Cold Vegetable Soup

# Cold Vegetable Soup
## (Gazpacho)

- 1   can (28 ounces) whole tomatoes
- 1   cup finely chopped green peppers
- 1   cup finely chopped cucumbers
- 1   cup croutons
- 1   medium onion, chopped (about 1/2 cup)
- 2   tablespoons white wine
- 2   tablespoons olive or vegetable oil
- 1   tablespoon ground cumin
- 1   tablespoon vinegar
- 1/2 teaspoon salt
- 1/4 teaspoon pepper

Place the tomatoes (with liquid), 1/2 cup of the green peppers, 1/2 cup of the cucumbers, 1/2 cup of the croutons, 1/4 cup of the onion, the wine, oil, cumin, vinegar, salt and pepper in blender container. Cover and blend on medium speed until smooth. Cover and refrigerate at least 1 hour. Serve with remaining ingredients as accompaniments. *8 servings (about 1/2 cup each).*

# Cream of Carrot Soup
## (Crema de Zanahoria)

- 1   small onion, chopped (about 1/4 cup)
- 2   tablespoons margarine or butter
- 2   cups chopped carrots (about 1 pound)
- 2   tablespoons white wine
- 3   cups Chicken Broth (page 26)
- 1   teaspoon salt
- 1/8 teaspoon ground nutmeg
     Dash of pepper
- 1   cup whipping cream

Cook and stir onion in margarine in 2-quart saucepan until tender. Add carrots and wine. Heat to boiling; reduce heat. Cover and simmer 10 minutes. Stir in Chicken Broth, salt, nutmeg and pepper. Heat to boiling; reduce heat. Cover and simmer until carrots are tender, 30 minutes.

Pour half the carrot mixture into blender container. Cover and blend on medium speed until smooth; strain. Repeat with remaining mixture. Heat until hot. Beat whipping cream until stiff; stir into soup. *6 servings (3/4 cup each).*

# Garlic Soup
## (Sopa de Ajo)

3   cloves garlic, crushed
2   tablespoons vegetable oil
2   slices white bread, cut into small pieces
4   cups Chicken Broth (page 26)
½   teaspoon salt
¼   teaspoon pepper
1   egg, slightly beaten

Cook and stir garlic in oil in 3-quart saucepan until brown. Add bread; cook and stir until light brown. Stir in Chicken Broth, salt and pepper. Heat to boiling; reduce heat. Cover and simmer 20 minutes. Stir at least half of the hot mixture gradually into egg. Blend into hot mixture in saucepan. Boil and stir 1 minute. Sprinkle with snipped parsley if desired. *8 servings (about ½ cup each).*

# Hot Broth
## (Caldo Tarasco)

1   tablespoon vegetable oil
4   Corn or Flour Tortillas (page 32),
        cut into thin strips
4   cups Chicken Broth (page 26)
½   cup Casera Sauce (page 65)
1   tablespoon finely chopped fully cooked smoked ham
1   dried chipotle pepper, finely chopped
    Juice of ½ lime (about 2 tablespoons)
    Snipped cilantro

Heat oil until hot. Cook and stir tortilla strips in hot oil until crisp. Heat Chicken Broth and Casera Sauce in 3-quart saucepan to boiling; reduce heat. Add tortilla strips, ham and chipotle pepper. Cover and simmer 5 minutes. Remove from heat; stir in lime juice. Sprinkle each serving with cilantro. *10 servings (½ cup each).*

# Tortillas, Eggs & Cheese

## Red Enchiladas with Cheese
### (Entomadas de Queso)

1 cup finely chopped onion
2 cloves garlic, finely chopped
1 cup vegetable oil
1 cup Chicken Broth (page 26)
8 tomatoes, chopped
1 tablespoon chili powder
1 teaspoon salt
1 teaspoon ground cumin
1 teaspoon dried oregano leaves
1/8 teaspoon pepper
12 Corn or Flour Tortillas (page 32)
3 cups shredded cheese (about 12 ounces)
Dairy sour cream

Cook and stir onion and garlic in oil in 12-inch skillet over medium heat until onion is tender. Stir in Chicken Broth, tomatoes, chili powder, salt, cumin, oregano and pepper. Heat to boiling; reduce heat. Simmer uncovered 1 hour.

Dip each tortilla into sauce to coat both sides. Spoon 2 tablespoons of the cheese onto each tortilla; roll tortilla around filling. Place seam sides down in ungreased rectangular baking dish, 13 × 9 × 2 inches. Pour remaining sauce over enchiladas; sprinkle with remaining cheese. Cook uncovered in 350° oven until cheese is melted, about 15 minutes. Serve with sour cream. *6 servings.*

## Green Enchiladas
### (Enchiladas Verdes)

12 Corn or Flour Tortillas (page 32)
2 cups Basic Green Sauce (page 64)
3 cups shredded cooked chicken, Refried Beans (page 79) or Minced Meat (page 51)
1 cup shredded Monterey Jack cheese (about 4 ounces)
Dairy sour cream

Heat each tortilla in ungreased skillet over medium heat, turning once, until soft, about 1 minute. Heat Green Sauce; dip each tortilla into sauce to coat both sides. Spoon 1/4 cup of the chicken onto each tortilla; roll tortilla around filling. Place seam sides down in ungreased rectangular baking dish, 13 × 9 × 2 inches. Pour remaining sauce over enchiladas; sprinkle with cheese. Cook uncovered in 350° oven until cheese is melted, 10 to 12 minutes. Serve with sour cream. *6 servings.*

*Red Enchiladas:* Substitute 2 cups Basic Red Sauce (page 65) for the Green Sauce. Substitute 3 cups shredded cheese or cooked beef for the chicken.

*Red Enchiladas with Cheese and Green Enchiladas*

# Corn Tortillas
## (Tortillas de Maíz)

Mix 2 cups masa harina and 1¼ cups warm water with hands until all masa harina is moistened and cleans side of bowl. (1 to 2 teaspoons water can be added if necessary.) Cover with damp towel; let rest 10 minutes. Divide into twelve 1-inch balls.

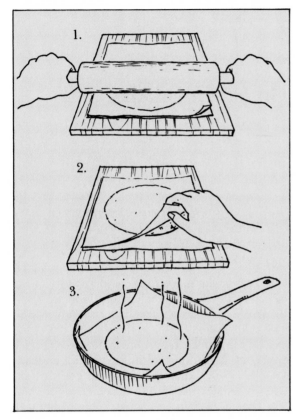

(1) Place each ball on waxed paper square; flatten slightly. Cover with second waxed paper square. Roll into 6-inch circle. (2) Peel off top square of waxed paper. Heat ungreased 10-inch skillet or griddle over medium-high heat until hot.

(3) Place each tortilla in skillet waxed paper side up; let cook about 30 seconds. Carefully remove waxed paper square. Cook tortilla until dry around edge, about 1 minute. Turn and cook other side until dry, about 2 minutes. Stack tortillas, placing waxed paper between each. Cover with a damp towel. *12 tortillas.*

*Note:* Purchased prepared 6-inch corn tortillas can be substituted in recipes calling for Corn Tortillas. Follow package directions for using tortillas.

# Flour Tortillas
## (Tortillas de Harina)

2   *cups all-purpose flour*
1   *teaspoon salt*
3   *tablespoons lard or shortening*
½   *cup warm water*

Cut lard into flour and salt until particles are size of small peas. Sprinkle in water, 1 tablespoon at a time, until all flour is moistened and dough almost cleans side of bowl. Gather dough into a ball; divide into 12 equal parts. Shape into balls; brush with lard. Cover and let rest 20 minutes.

Roll each ball on floured surface into 6-inch circle. Heat ungreased 8-inch skillet or griddle over medium-high heat until hot. Cook tortilla until dry around edge and blisters appear on surface, about 2 minutes. Turn and cook other side until dry, about 1 minute. Stack tortillas, placing waxed paper between each. Cover with a damp towel. *12 tortillas.*

*Note:* Purchased prepared 6-inch flour tortillas can be substituted in recipes calling for Flour Tortillas. Follow package directions for using tortillas.

# Turnovers
## (Empanadas)

Prepare Flour Tortillas (opposite); omit cooking step. Spoon about 2 tablespoons shredded cheese, Minced Meat (page 51) or Refried Beans (page 79) onto half of round.

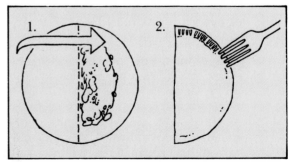

(1) Fold other half over filling. (2) Seal with fork. Heat oil (1 inch) to 365°. Fry turnovers until golden brown, turning once, about 3 minutes. Drain on paper towels. *12 turnovers.*

# Tortilla Skillet
## (Chilaquiles)

12   Corn or Flour Tortillas (page 32)
½   cup vegetable oil
½   cup chopped scallions or green onions (with tops)
1   can (16 ounces) whole tomatoes, drained
½   teaspoon ground oregano
½   teaspoon salt
⅛   teaspoon pepper
1   cup shredded Monterey Jack cheese
   Dairy sour cream

Cut tortillas into thin strips. Heat oil in 10-inch skillet until hot. Cook tortillas and scallions, turning occasionally, until tortillas are crisp, about 10 minutes. Stir in tomatoes, oregano, salt and pepper. Sprinkle with cheese; heat just until cheese is melted. Serve with sour cream. *4 to 6 servings.*

# Turkey and Tortilla Casserole
## (Caserola de Pavo y Tortilla)

12   Flour Tortillas (page 32)
2   cups Basic Green Sauce (page 64)
2   cups cut-up cooked turkey or chicken
2   cups shredded cheese (about 8 ounces)
   Dairy sour cream

Dip each tortilla into warm Basic Green Sauce to coat both sides. Place 4 of the tortillas in 9-inch pie plate with edges overlapping. Top with 1 cup of the turkey. Add 4 tortillas; sprinkle with 1 cup of the cheese. Top with remaining tortillas. Arrange remaining turkey on top; pour remaining sauce over turkey. Sprinkle with remaining cheese. Cook uncovered in 350° oven until cheese is melted, about 20 minutes. Serve with sour cream. Sprinkle with paprika if desired. *6 to 8 servings.*

# Mixed Tostadas
## (Tostadas Compuestas)

1½  cups Refried Beans (page 79)
1½  cups Casera Sauce (page 65)
    Vegetable oil
  6  Corn Tortillas (page 32)
  2  cups cut-up cooked chicken or shredded
      cooked beef
  ¾  cup shredded Monterey Jack cheese
      (about 3 ounces)
  3  cups shredded lettuce
  1  avocado, cut into 12 slices
    Dairy sour cream

Heat Refried Beans and Casera Sauce. Heat ⅛ inch oil in 8-inch skillet over medium heat just until hot. Cook tortillas, 1 at a time, in hot oil until crisp, about 1 minute. Drain on paper towels.

Spread each tortilla with ¼ cup of the beans. Top with 2 tablespoons of the sauce, ⅓ cup of the chicken and 2 tablespoons of the sauce. Sprinkle each with 2 tablespoons of the cheese. Set oven control to broil and/or 550°. Broil with tops 2 to 3 inches from heat until cheese is melted, about 3 minutes. Top each with ½ cup lettuce and 2 avocado slices. Garnish with sour cream. *6 servings.*

# Soft Tacos
## (Tacos)

Prepare Corn Tortillas (page 32). Heat ⅛ inch vegetable oil until hot. Heat each tortilla in oil until soft, about 30 seconds. Drain on paper towels. Spoon 2 tablespoons shredded cooked beef, shredded cooked pork, shredded cooked chicken or Minced Meat (page 51) slightly below center of tortilla. Roll tortilla over filling and secure with wooden pick.

Heat ⅛ inch vegetable oil until hot. Fry each taco until light golden brown, turning once, about 2 minutes. Drain on paper towels. Remove wooden picks. Garnish with 2 or 3 of the following: chopped tomatoes, shredded lettuce, chopped onion, chopped green chilies, chopped avocado and shredded cheese. *6 servings.*

# Beef Burritos
## (Burritos de Res)

    Flour Tortillas (page 32)
  2  cups shredded cooked beef
  1  cup Refried Beans (page 79)
  2  cups shredded lettuce
  2  medium tomatoes, chopped
  1  cup shredded cheese (about 4 ounces)

Prepare Flour Tortillas as directed except divide dough into 8 equal parts. Roll each into 10-inch circle on floured surface. Cook as directed in ungreased 10-inch skillet or griddle.

Heat 1 tortilla in ungreased 10-inch skillet or on griddle over medium-high heat, turning frequently, until hot and pliable, about 1 minute. Place about ¼ cup of the beef slightly below center of tortilla. Spoon about 2 tablespoons Refried Beans on beef. Top with ¼ cup of the lettuce and about 2 tablespoons each of the tomatoes and cheese.

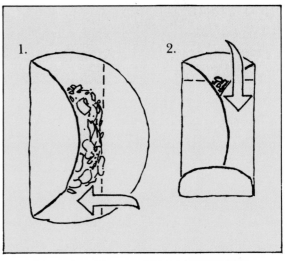

(1) Fold 2 opposite sides of tortilla over filling. (2) Fold remaining open edges over folded edges. Repeat with remaining tortillas. *8 servings.*

*Fried Burritos:* Prepare as directed above except omit lettuce and cheese in filling. Heat oil (about 1 inch) to 365°. Fry Burritos until golden brown, turning once, about 2 minutes. Top with shredded lettuce and cheese.

*Minced Meat Burritos:* Substitute ½ cup Minced Meat (page 51) for the beef, refried beans, lettuce, tomatoes and cheese.

*Filled Tortillas*

# Filled Tortillas
## (Panuchos)

1　medium onion, thinly sliced
4　radishes, thinly sliced
2　tablespoons vinegar
1　tablespoon orange juice concentrate
6　drops red pepper sauce
½　teaspoon salt
　　Flour Tortillas (page 32)
2　cups Refried Beans (page 79)
　　Vegetable oil
2　cups shredded lettuce
2　cups shredded cooked chicken
2　jalapeno peppers, thinly sliced
2　tomatoes, sliced

Mix onion, radishes, vinegar, orange juice concentrate, pepper sauce and salt in glass or plastic bowl. Cover and refrigerate 30 minutes; drain. Prepare Flour Tortillas as directed in recipe except divide into 6 equal parts.

(1) Carefully split each tortilla with a knife to form a pocket. (2) Spread 2 tablespoons Refried Beans in each pocket; close pockets. Heat oil (1½ inches) to

365°. Fry tortillas, 1 at a time, until crisp and golden brown, about 1 minute on each side. Drain on paper towels. Top each with shredded lettuce, onion mixture, chicken, jalapeno peppers and tomatoes. *6 servings.*

## Festival Eggs
## (Huevos de Fiesta)

1/4 cup margarine or butter
1/4 cup vegetable oil
6 Corn or Flour Tortillas (page 32),
    cut into thin strips
1 medium onion, chopped (about 1/2 cup)
6 eggs, beaten
2 tomatoes, chopped
1 jalapeno pepper, seeded and chopped
2 tablespoons snipped cilantro
3/4 teaspoon salt
1/4 teaspoon pepper
1/2 cup shredded cheese (about 2 ounces)

Heat margarine and oil in 10-inch skillet over medium heat until hot. Add tortilla strips and onion; cook, turning occasionally, until tortillas are brown. Mix remaining ingredients except cheese; pour into skillet.

As mixture begins to set at bottom and side, gently lift cooked portion with spatula so that thin uncooked portion can flow to bottom. Turn egg mixture; cook just until eggs are set but not dry. Sprinkle with cheese. *6 servings.*

## Broiled Bean Sandwiches
## (Molletes)

6 French rolls
1 1/2 cups Refried Beans (page 79)
3/4 cup shredded cheese (about 3 ounces)

Cut rolls lengthwise into halves. Set oven control to broil and/or 550°. Broil halves until golden brown. Spread each half with 2 tablespoons Refried Beans. Sprinkle each with 1 tablespoon cheese. Broil with tops 2 to 3 inches from heat until cheese is melted, about 1 1/2 minutes. Serve with egg dishes or as a snack. *12 sandwiches.*

## Mexican Omelet
## (Omelete a la Mexicana)

2 eggs
2 tablespoons half-and-half
1/2 teaspoon dried oregano leaves
1/4 teaspoon salt
    Dash of pepper
1 tablespoon margarine or butter
1/4 cup shredded cheese (about 1 ounce)
2 tablespoons chopped green chilies
    Casera Sauce (page 65)
    Dairy sour cream

Mix eggs, half-and-half, oregano, salt and pepper with fork just until whites and yolks are blended. Heat margarine in 8-inch skillet or omelet pan over medium-high heat. As margarine melts, tilt skillet in all directions to coat side thoroughly. When margarine just begins to brown, skillet is hot enough to use.

Quickly pour eggs all at once into skillet. Start sliding skillet back and forth rapidly over heat. At the same time, stir quickly with fork to spread eggs continuously over bottom of skillet as they thicken. Let stand over heat a few seconds to lightly brown bottom of omelet.(Do not overcook — omelet will continue to cook after folding.)

Tilt skillet; run fork under edge of omelet, then jerk skillet sharply to loosen eggs from bottom of skillet. Sprinkle with cheese and green chilies. Fold portion of omelet nearest you just to center. (Allow for portion of omelet to slide up side of skillet.)

Grasp skillet handle; turn omelet onto warm plate, flipping folded portion of omelet over so far side is on bottom. Tuck sides of omelet under if necessary. Top with Casera Sauce and sour cream; sprinkle with snipped cilantro if desired. *1 serving.*

*Broiled Bean Sandwiches and Mexican Omelet*

# Poached Eggs, Yucatan Style
## (Huevos Yucatecos)

1   small onion, chopped (about ¼ cup)
2   tablespoons margarine or butter
1   tablespoon vegetable oil
2   tomatoes, chopped
1   jalapeno pepper, seeded and finely chopped
2   tablespoons snipped cilantro
4   eggs
    Salt and pepper
½   cup toasted pumpkin seeds, ground

Cook and stir onion in margarine and oil in 10-inch skillet until tender. Add tomatoes, jalapeno pepper and cilantro. Cover and simmer 10 minutes.

Break each egg into measuring cup or saucer; holding cup close to sauce's surface, slip 1 egg at a time onto sauce. Cover and cook until desired doneness, 3 to 5 minutes. Season with salt and pepper; sprinkle with pumpkin seeds. *4 servings.*

# Eggs Yucatan Style
## (Huevos Motulenos)

¼   cup vegetable oil
8   Corn Tortillas (page 32)
½   cup finely chopped onion
2   medium tomatoes, chopped
2   cloves garlic, finely chopped
1½  teaspoons ground oregano
1   teaspoon salt
⅛   teaspoon pepper
1   cup Refried Beans (page 79)
4   fried eggs
1½  cups finely chopped fully cooked smoked ham
½   cup cooked green peas
1   cup shredded cheese (about 4 ounces)

Heat oil in 8-inch skillet over medium-low heat just until hot. Cook tortillas, 1 at a time, in hot oil a few seconds on each side. Drain on paper towels. Pour all but 2 tablespoons oil from skillet. Cook and stir onion in oil until tender. Add tomatoes, garlic, oregano, salt and pepper. Simmer uncovered until thickened, about 10 minutes. Spread each of 4 tortillas with ¼ cup Refried Beans.

Place an egg on each bean-covered tortilla. Top with 2 tablespoons tomato mixture; cover with another tortilla and 2 tablespoons tomato mixture. Sprinkle each with ham, peas and cheese. *4 servings.*

*Poached Eggs Yucatan Style and Eggs with Sardines*

# Eggs with Sardines
## (Huevos Potosinos)

12  hard-cooked eggs
1   can (4³/₈ ounces) sardines, drained
    Juice of ½ lime (about 2 tablespoons)
⅛  teaspoon freshly ground pepper
¼  cup margarine or butter
2   tablespoons flour
½  teaspoon salt
2   cups milk
1   cup cooked green peas
2   tablespoons snipped parsley
1   cup shredded cheese (about 4 ounces)
1   cup sliced pimiento-stuffed olives

Cut peeled eggs lengthwise into halves. Slip out yolks; mash yolks and sardines with fork. Stir in lime juice and pepper. Fill whites with egg yolk mixture, heaping lightly.

Heat margarine over low heat until melted. Stir in flour and salt. Cook over low heat, stirring constantly, until mixture is smooth and bubbly; remove from heat. Stir in milk. Heat to boiling, stirring constantly. Boil and stir 1 minute. Stir in peas and parsley. Pour sauce over eggs; sprinkle with cheese and olives. *6 to 8 servings.*

# Eggs Sonora Style
## (Huevos Sonorenses)

2   tablespoons vegetable oil
6   Flour Tortillas (page 32)
³/₄  cup Refried Beans (page 79)
6   poached eggs
³/₄  cup Casera Sauce (page 65)
1   tablespoon finely chopped fully cooked smoked ham
³/₄  cup shredded cheese (about 3 ounces)

Heat vegetable oil in 8-inch skillet over medium-low heat just until hot. Cook tortillas, 1 at a time, in hot oil a few seconds on each side. Drain on paper towels. Spread 2 tablespoons Refried Beans on each tortilla.

Place an egg on each tortilla. Mix Casera Sauce and ham; spoon about 2 tablespoons over each egg. Sprinkle each with 2 tablespoons cheese. Set oven control to broil and/or 550°. Broil with tops 3 to 5 inches from heat until cheese is melted, about 1 minute. *6 servings.*

# Eggs and Sausage
## (Huevos con Chorizo)

2   Spiced Sausage (page 51)
1   small onion, chopped (about ¼ cup)
2   tablespoons vegetable oil
8   eggs
¼   cup half-and-half
½   teaspoon dried oregano leaves

Remove casings from sausage; chop sausage finely. Cook and stir onion in oil in 10-inch skillet until tender. Add sausage. Cook and stir sausage until firm; drain. Return to skillet.

Mix eggs, half-and-half and oregano with fork, stirring thoroughly for a uniform yellow. Pour egg mixture into skillet. As mixture begins to set at bottom and side, gently lift cooked portion with spatula so that thin uncooked portion can flow to bottom. Avoid constant stirring. Cook until eggs are thickened throughout but still moist, 3 to 5 minutes. *4 to 6 servings.*

---

### ABOUT TORTILLAS

The tortilla is the basic bread of Mexico and is made from flour or corn. They are good eaten warm and spread with butter. Tortillas can be cut into strips, fried and used in main dishes or soups. They are often cut into wedges, fried until crisp and served with dips.

In Mexico, *tacos* are always made with the soft tortillas; the crisp tortilla shell is the American version. *Enchiladas* are rolled, filled tortillas covered with a sauce and heated in the oven. *Burritos* are always made with flour tortillas rather than corn tortillas. They can also be fried until crisp, however, this is more popular in California and southwestern United States than in Mexico. *Tostadas* are to Mexican cuisine what hamburgers are to that of the United States. Every region of Mexico has its variation of this open-faced "sandwich".

# Ranch Style Eggs
## (Huevos Rancheros)

3    Spiced Sausage (page 51)
     Vegetable oil
6    Corn Tortillas (page 32)
1¼   cups warm Casera Sauce (page 65)
6    fried eggs
1½   cups shredded cheese (about 6 ounces)

Remove casings from sausage. Cook and stir sausage until crumbled and firm; drain. Heat ⅛ inch oil in 8-inch skillet over medium heat just until hot. Cook tortillas, 1 at a time, in hot oil until crisp, about 1 minute. Drain on paper towels.

Spread each tortilla with 1 tablespoon sauce to soften. Place an egg on each tortilla. Top each egg with scant tablespoon sauce, ¼ cup crumbled Spiced Sausage, another tablespoon sauce and ¼ cup cheese. *6 servings.*

---

# Egg and Potato Scramble
## (Huevos a la Española)

2    cups diced uncooked potatoes
1    bay leaf
1    medium onion, chopped (about ½ cup)
¼    cup margarine or butter
1    cup chopped fully cooked smoked ham
6    eggs, beaten
½    teaspoon salt
¼    teaspoon pepper

Heat 1 inch salted water (½ teaspoon salt to 1 cup water) to boiling. Add potatoes and bay leaf. Cover and cook until potatoes are tender, about 10 minutes; drain. Cook and stir onion in margarine in 10-inch skillet until tender. Add potatoes. Cook and stir until golden brown. Stir in ham.

Mix eggs, salt and pepper; pour into skillet. As mixture begins to set at bottom and side, gently lift cooked portion wth spatula so that thin uncooked portion can flow to bottom. Avoid constant stirring. Cook until eggs are thickened throughout but still moist, 3 to 5 minutes. *4 servings.*

# Egg and Spinach Casserole
## (Huevos a la Espinaca)

　　*Vegetable oil*
6　*Corn Tortillas (page 32)*
1　*small onion, chopped (about ¼ cup)*
2　*slices bacon, cut up*
1　*clove garlic, finely chopped*
2　*tablespoons margarine or butter*
1　*tablespoon vegetable oil*
2　*tomatoes, chopped*
1　*teaspoon salt*
½　*teaspoon pepper*
¼　*teaspoon ground nutmeg*
1　*pound spinach, chopped*
8　*hard-cooked eggs*
1　*cup Basic Green Sauce (page 64)*
1　*cup shredded cheese (about 4 ounces)*

Heat ⅛ inch oil in 8-inch skillet over medium heat, just until hot. Cook tortillas, 1 at a time, in hot oil until crisp, about 1 minute. Drain on paper towels. Cut into small pieces. Cook and stir onion, bacon and garlic in margarine and oil in 10-inch skillet until onion is tender. Stir in tomatoes, salt, pepper and nutmeg. Simmer uncovered 3 minutes. Add spinach; cover and cook until spinach is wilted, about 3 minutes.

Line bottom of ungreased square pan, 8 × 8 × 2 inches, with fried tortilla pieces. Spread spinach mixture over tortilla pieces. Cut eggs lengthwise into halves; arrange on spinach. Pour Green Sauce over eggs; sprinkle with cheese. Cook uncovered in 400° oven until cheese is melted, about 15 minutes. *8 servings.*

# Stuffed Chilies
## (Chiles Rellenos)

8　*poblano peppers*
2　*cups shredded cheese (about 8 ounces)*
1　*cup dry bread crumbs*
4　*eggs, separated*
¼　*teaspoon salt*
¼　*teaspoon cream of tartar*
　　*Vegetable oil*
1　*cup tomato juice*
½　*cup Casera Sauce (page 65)*
1　*tablespoon finely chopped fully cooked smoked ham*
　　*Dairy sour cream*
　　*Snipped cilantro*

Set oven control to broil and/or 550°. Place poblano peppers on rack in broiler pan. Broil peppers 4 to 5 inches from heat until skins blister, about 5 minutes on each side. Wrap in towels; let stand 5 minutes. Peel peppers carefully, starting at stem end. Cut a slit lengthwise down side of each pepper. Carefully remove seeds and membranes; rinse. Fill each pepper with ¼ cup cheese; coat with bread crumbs. Cover and refrigerate 20 minutes.

Beat egg whites, salt and cream of tartar until stiff. Beat egg yolks until thick and lemon colored, about 5 minutes; fold into egg whites. Heat vegetable oil (1 to 1½ inches) to 375°. Dip each pepper into egg mixture. Fry 1 pepper at a time, turning once, until puffy and golden brown, about 3 minutes. Place peppers on paper towels on cookie sheet; keep warm in 200° oven.

Heat tomato juice, Casera Sauce and ham to boiling. Pour over peppers. Garnish with sour cream and cilantro. *8 servings.*

# Seafood & Poultry

## Baked Red Snapper
## (Huachinango al Horno)

1   cup milk
1   teaspoon dried oregano leaves
2   pounds red snapper fillets, cut into 8 pieces
1   medium onion, sliced
1/4  cup olive or vegetable oil
4   tomatoes, chopped
2   cloves garlic, finely chopped
2   tablespoons capers
1/2  cup pitted olives
1/4  cup dry white wine
    Juice of 1 lemon (about 1/4 cup)
1   teaspoon salt
1   teaspoon ground cumin
1/4  teaspoon pepper

Mix milk and oregano; pour over fish. Cover and refrigerate 1 hour. Cook and stir onion in oil in 10-inch skillet until tender. Stir in remaining ingredients except fish. Simmer uncovered until thickened, about 15 minutes. Drain fish; pat dry with paper towels.

Place 1 fish fillet on each of eight 12-inch heavy-duty aluminum foil squares. Divide sauce among fish. Fold foil over fish; seal securely. Place packets in ungreased jelly roll pan, 15½ × 10½ × 1 inch. Cook in 350° oven until fish flakes easily with fork, 30 minutes. Sprinkle with snipped cilantro and serve with lemon wedges if desired. *8 servings.*

## Sea Bass in Cilantro
## (Robalo al Cilantro)

1   cup milk
1   teaspoon ground cumin
2   pounds bass or red snapper fillets, cut into 8 pieces
1   cup finely chopped onion
1/4  cup vegetable oil
1/4  to 1/2 cup snipped cilantro
1   cup finely chopped green chilies
1½  teaspoons salt
1/4  teaspoon pepper
    Lime or lemon wedges

Mix milk and cumin; pour over fish. Cover and refrigerate 1 hour. Cook and stir onion in oil in 2-quart saucepan until tender. Stir in remaining ingredients except fish and lime wedges. Heat to boiling; reduce heat. Simmer uncovered until thickened, about 10 minutes.

Drain fish; pat dry with paper towels. Place 1 fish fillet on each of eight 12-inch heavy-duty aluminum foil squares. Divide sauce among fish. Fold foil over fish; seal securely. Place packets in ungreased jelly roll pan, 15½ × 10½ × 1 inch. Cook in 350° oven until fish flakes easily with fork, 25 to 30 minutes. Serve with lime wedges. *8 servings*

*Baked Red Snapper*

# Shrimp Veracruz
## (Camarones a la Veracruzana)

1  pound fresh or frozen shrimp
2  tablespoons margarine or butter
2  tablespoons vegetable oil
1  cup Casera Sauce (page 65)
1  tablespoon chopped fully cooked smoked ham

Peel shrimp. (If shrimp is frozen, do not thaw; peel under running cold water.) Make a shallow cut down back of each shrimp; wash out sand vein. Cut shrimp lengthwise almost into halves.

Heat margarine and oil in 10-inch skillet until hot. Cook and stir shrimp 1 minute. Add Casera Sauce and ham. Heat to boiling; reduce heat. Simmer uncovered until shrimp are pink, about 2 minutes. Garnish with snipped cilantro and lemon wedges if desired. *4 servings.*

# Rice and Seafood
## (Paella)

1  cup uncooked regular rice
1/4  cup olive or vegetable oil
2  Spiced Sausage (page 51), cooked and sliced
1  cup Chicken Broth (page 26)
1  cup clam juice
1  cup green peas
1/2  cup chopped carrots
   Dash of ground saffron
16  mussels (in shells)
8  clams (in shells)
8  fresh or frozen raw shrimp (in shells)

Cook and stir rice in oil in 4-quart Dutch oven until golden brown. Stir in Spiced Sausage, Chicken Broth, clam juice, peas, carrots and saffron. Place remaining ingredients on top of rice mixture. Heat to boiling; reduce heat. Cover and simmer 20 minutes. (Do not lift cover or stir.) Garnish with snipped cilantro and lemon wedges if desired. *8 servings.*

# Cod with Garlic
## (Bacalao al Mojo de Ajo)

2  pounds cod or scrod fillets
8  cloves garlic, finely chopped
2  tablespoons margarine or butter
2  tablespoons vegetable oil
   Juice of 1 lemon (about 1/4 cup)
1  teaspoon salt
   Snipped cilantro

Cut fish into 8 serving pieces; place on rack in broiler pan. Cook and stir garlic in margarine and oil until golden brown. Remove garlic with slotted spoon; reserve. Drizzle the margarine mixture and lemon juice over fish; sprinkle with salt.

Set oven control to broil and/or 550°. Broil with tops 2 to 3 inches from heat until fish flakes easily with fork, 10 to 12 minutes. Sprinkle with reserved garlic and the cilantro. Serve with lemon wedges if desired. *8 servings.*

# Shrimp Cilantro
## (Camarones al Cilantro)

16  large fresh or frozen raw shrimp
1  medium onion, chopped (about 1/2 cup)
2  cloves garlic, finely chopped
2  tablespoons margarine or butter
2  tablespoons vegetable oil
2  tablespoons snipped cilantro
   Lemon slices

Peel shrimp. (If shrimp is frozen, do not thaw; peel under cold water.) Make a shallow cut down back of each shrimp; wash out sand vein. Cook and stir onion and garlic in margarine and oil in 10-inch skillet until tender. Add shrimp; cook 1 minute. Turn; cook until pink, about 2 minutes. (Do not overcook.) Sprinkle with cilantro. Pour pan juices over shrimp; garnish with lemon. *4 servings.*

# Stuffed Squid in Chile Sauce
## (Calamares Rellenos)

>      Chipotle Sauce (page 53)
> 2    pounds squid
> 1/4  cup finely chopped onion
> 1/2  cup vegetable oil
> 3/4  cup dry bread crumbs
> 1/2  cup red wine
> 1/4  cup finely chopped carrot
> 1/4  cup finely chopped celery
> 1/4  cup snipped parsley
> 2    cloves garlic, finely chopped
> 2    anchovy fillets, mashed
> 1/2  cup all-purpose flour
> 1/2  cup vegetable oil
> 1    cup clam juice
>      Hot cooked rice

Prepare Chipotle Sauce. Separate the heads from the tails of the squid by carefully pulling apart. Cut tentacles from head sections just before eyes; discard head sections. Remove and discard the cartilage from the base of the tentacles and the transparent pen from the tail cones. Wash tentacles and tail cones under running cold water; pat dry with paper towels. Chop tentacles finely.

Cook and stir onion in 1/2 cup oil in 10-inch skillet until tender. Add tentacles, bread crumbs, wine, carrot, celery, parsley, garlic and anchovies. Toss lightly; heat until hot. Fill pockets of tail cone with stuffing. Secure openings with wooden picks. Coat with flour.

Heat 1/2 cup oil until hot. Cook squid over medium heat until brown on all sides; drain on paper towels. Drain fat from skillet; heat Chipotle Sauce and clam juice to boiling. Add squid; reduce heat. Simmer uncovered 30 minutes. Serve on rice. Garnish with snipped cilantro and lemon wedges if desired. *6 or 7 servings.*

# Fried Squid Rings
## (Calamares Fritos)

> 2    pounds squid
>      Juice of 1 lime (about 1/4 cup)
>      Vegetable oil
> 1    cup all-purpose flour
> 4    eggs, slightly beaten
> 2    cups dry bread crumbs
>      Salt
>      Lemon wedges

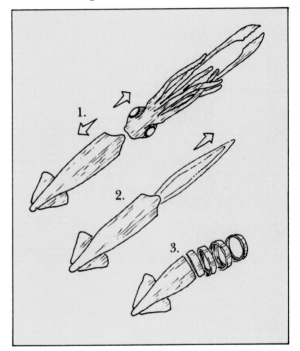

(1) Separate the heads from the tails of the squid by carefully pulling apart; discard head sections. (2) Remove the transparent pen from the tail cones. Wash tail cones under running cold water; drain. (3) Cut tail cones into 1/4-inch slices; place in glass or plastic bowl. Add just enough water to cover and the lime juice. Cover and refrigerate 1 hour.

Heat oil (1 1/2 to 2 inches) to 375°. Drain squid; pat dry with paper towels. Coat squid with flour; dip into eggs, then coat with bread crumbs. Fry until golden brown, about 1 minute. Drain on paper towels. Sprinkle with salt; serve with lemon wedges. Garnish with snipped cilantro if desired. *8 servings.*

*Chicken Cilantro*

# Chicken Cilantro
## (Pollo al Cilantro)

1   small onion, chopped (about ¼ cup)
1   clove garlic, finely chopped
2   tablespoons margarine or butter
2   tablespoons vegetable oil
4   chicken breasts, boned, skinned and cut
        into 1-inch pieces
1   teaspoon salt
¼   teaspoon pepper
2   tablespoons snipped cilantro

Cook and stir onion and garlic in margarine and oil in 10-inch skillet until onion is tender. Add chicken, salt and pepper. Cook and stir over medium-high heat until done, about 5 minutes; stir in cilantro. Pour pan juices over chicken to serve. Garnish with lemon wedge if desired. *4 servings.*

# Chicken in Mole Sauce
## (Mole Poblano)

½   cup lard or shortening
¼   cup chili powder
2   cups Chicken Broth (page 26)
12  Flour Tortillas (page 32), cut into small pieces
½   cup tomato sauce
1   medium onion, chopped (about ½ cup)
2   cloves garlic, finely chopped
1   or 2 chipotle peppers, finely chopped
2   tablespoons raisins
2   tablespoons chopped almonds or walnuts
2   tablespoons sesame seed
2   tablespoons pumpkin seeds
2   tablespoons peanut butter
1   tablespoon sugar
1   tablespoon ground oregano
1   tablespoon cocoa
1   teaspoon anise seed
½   teaspoon ground cinnamon
½   teaspoon ground cloves
½   teaspoon ground nutmeg
½   teaspoon ground allspice
½   teaspoon ground ginger
½   teaspoon ground cumin or 1 teaspoon cumin seed
2   cups Chicken Broth (page 26)
8   chicken breasts, boned

Heat lard in 12-inch skillet over medium heat until hot. Cook and stir chili powder in lard until brown. (Add about ½ teaspoon water to prevent scorching if necessary.) Cool. Stir in 2 cups of the Chicken Broth. Add remaining ingredients except 2 cups broth and the chicken. Heat to boiling; reduce heat. Simmer uncovered 1 hour. Cool.

Pour a small amount of sauce at a time into blender container. Cover and blend on high speed until smooth. Heat 2 cups of the sauce and the remaining broth to boiling in 12-inch skillet; reduce heat. Arrange chicken skin sides up in single layer in skillet. Cover and simmer until done, about 1 hour. Add remaining sauce; heat until hot. *8 servings.*

## Chicken Almendrado
### (Pollo Almendrado)

1    medium onion, chopped (about ½ cup)
2    tablespoons margarine or butter
1    tablespoon vegetable oil
1    cup Chicken Broth (page 26)
¼    cup slivered almonds
1    tablespoon chili powder
1    teaspoon vinegar
½    teaspoon sugar
½    teaspoon ground cinnamon
4    chicken breasts, boned
     Slivered almonds

Cook and stir onion in margarine and oil in 10-inch skillet until tender. Stir in Chicken Broth, ¼ cup almonds, the chili powder, vinegar, sugar and cinnamon. Heat to boiling; reduce heat. Simmer uncovered 10 minutes.

Transfer to blender container; cover and blend on low speed until smooth, about 1 minute. Return sauce to skillet. Dip chicken into sauce to coat both sides. Arrange chicken skin sides up in single layer in skillet. Heat to boiling; reduce heat. Cover and simmer until done, about 45 minutes. Pour sauce over chicken; sprinkle with almonds. *4 servings.*

## Mexican Chicken
### (Pollo a la Mexicana)

1    medium onion, thinly sliced
½    cup vegetable oil
4    tomatoes, chopped
½    cup water
12   pitted green olives
2    stalks celery, chopped
2    tablespoons capers
2    cloves garlic, finely chopped
2    bay leaves
1    tablespoon dried oregano leaves
1    teaspoon salt
¼    teaspoon pepper
6    chicken breasts, boned
8    ounces mushrooms, sliced

Cook and stir onion in oil in 10-inch skillet until tender. Stir in remaining ingredients except chicken and mushrooms. Heat to boiling; reduce heat. Simmer uncovered 30 minutes. Arrange chicken skin sides up in single layer in skillet; cover and cook 30 minutes. Add mushrooms; cover and cook until chicken is done, about 15 minutes longer. *6 servings.*

# Beef & Pork

## Beef and Plantains
### (Cocido de Carne de Res con Plátano)

|   | Vegetable oil |
|---|---|
| 2 | plantains, cut into 1/4-inch slices |
| 1 | teaspoon chili powder |
| 2 | pounds beef for stew |
| 4 | cups water |
| 4 | tomatoes, chopped |
| 2 | medium onions, each cut into fourths |
| 1/4 | cup chopped celery |
| 1/4 | cup chopped carrot |
| 2 | cloves garlic |
| 8 | whole cloves |
| 2 | tablespoons snipped cilantro |
| 2 | teaspoons salt |
| 1 | teaspoon ground thyme |
| 1 | teaspoon ground oregano |
| 1/4 | teaspoon pepper |
| 1 | cup chopped green pepper |

Heat oil (1 inch) to 350°. Fry plantains in hot oil until golden brown, about 2 minutes. Drain on paper towels; toss with chili powder. Cut beef into 1-inch pieces. Heat all ingredients except plantains and green pepper to boiling in 4-quart Dutch oven; reduce heat. Cover and simmer until beef is tender 2 to 2½ hours.

Drain beef; reserve broth. Cook reserved broth uncovered over high heat until reduced to 3 cups. Add beef mixture, plantains and green pepper to broth. Simmer uncovered 10 minutes. Serve with Mexican Rice (page 78) if desired. 6 to 8 servings.

## Mexican Pot Roast
### (Asado a la Mexicana)

| 6 | pound beef arm, blade or cross rib pot roast |
|---|---|
| 8 | cloves garlic |
| 4 | slices bacon, cut into halves |
| 2 | teaspoons salt |
| 1/2 | teaspoon ground pepper |
| 1/2 | cup prepared mustard |
| 1/4 | cup vegetable oil |
| 1 | medium onion, chopped (about 1/2 cup) |
| 1 | bottle (12 ounces) beer |
| 2 | bay leaves |
| 2 | tablespoons snipped cilantro |
| 1 | teaspoon ground nutmeg |
| 1 | teaspoon ground thyme |
| 1/2 | cup chopped carrots |
| 1/2 | cup chopped celery |
| 1/2 | cup sliced mushrooms |
| 2 | jalapeno peppers, seeded and finely chopped |

Make a cut 1½ inches deep across beef. Wrap each clove garlic in 1 piece bacon; insert into cut. Sprinkle beef with salt and pepper; spread with mustard. Cover and refrigerate at least 4 hours.

Cook beef in oil in 4-quart Dutch oven over medium heat until brown. Add remaining ingredients. Heat to boiling; reduce heat. Cover and cook until tender, about 2½ hours. Remove beef to warm platter. Skim fat from broth. Place 2 cups of the broth in blender. Blend on medium speed until smooth. Serve with beef. *12 servings.*

*Beef and Plantains and Mexican Rice, page 78*

*Stuffed Flank Steak*

# Stuffed Flank Steak
## (Matambre)

1½  pound beef flank steak
¾  cup red wine
1  clove garlic, finely chopped
1  tablespoon snipped parsley
1½  teaspoons salt
½  teaspoon ground oregano
½  teaspoon ground thyme
1  small onion, chopped (about ¼ cup)
2  tablespoons margarine or butter
¼  cup chopped carrot
¼  cup chopped mushrooms
½  cup dry bread crumbs
3  hard-cooked eggs
2  tablespoons vegetable oil
1  cup Beef Broth (page 26)
1  jalapeno pepper, seeded and finely chopped
¼  cup chopped celery
¼  cup dry white wine
1  tablespoon cornstarch

Split beef lengthwise almost into halves; open and place in shallow glass or plastic dish. Mix wine, garlic, parsley, salt, oregano and thyme; pour over beef. Cover and refrigerate at least 1 hour. Drain; reserve marinade.

Cook and stir onion in margarine in 2-quart saucepan until tender. Add reserved marinade, the carrot and mushrooms. Heat to boiling; cook uncovered 10 minutes. Stir in bread crumbs. Spread mixture on opened beef to within 1 inch of edge. Place 3 eggs along narrow end. Roll up, beginning at narrow end; secure with wooden picks.

Cook beef in 2 tablespoons oil until brown; drain. Add Beef Broth, jalapeno pepper and celery. Heat to boiling; reduce heat. Cover and simmer until beef is tender, about 1 hour. Remove beef to warm platter; remove wooden picks. Mix wine and cornstarch; stir gradually into broth mixture. Heat to boiling, stirring constantly. Boil and stir 1 minute. Cut beef into slices; serve with sauce. *6 servings.*

# Broiled Steak
## (Carne Asada)

2  1- to 1½-pound high-quality beef flank steaks
   Juice of 2 limes (about ½ cup)
2  tablespoons dried oregano leaves
2  tablespoons olive or vegetable oil
2  teaspoons salt
½  teaspoon pepper
4  cloves garlic, crushed

Place beef steaks in shallow glass pan. Mix remaining ingredients; pour over beef. Cover and refrigerate at least 8 hours, turning beef occasionally.

Set oven control to broil and/or 550°. Broil beef with tops 2 to 3 inches from heat until brown, about 5 minutes. Turn beef; broil 5 minutes. Cut beef across grain at slanted angle into thin slices. Serve wth tortillas and guacamole if desired. *8 servings.*

# Minced Meat
## (Picadillo)

1   medium onion, chopped (about ½ cup)
2   tablespoons vegetable oil
1   can (16 ounces) stewed tomatoes
3   cups shredded cooked beef
¾   cup chopped green olives
½   cup raisins
2   cloves garlic, finely chopped
1   tablespoon capers
1   teaspoon dried oregano leaves

Cook and stir chopped onion in oil in 10-inch skillet until tender. Add stewed tomatoes; cover and simmer 5 minutes. Stir in beef, olives, raisins, garlic, capers and oregano. Cover and simmer 15 minutes. Serve with rice if desired. *6 servings.*

# Beef and Tequila Stew
## (Cocido de Carne de Res con Tequila)

2    pounds beef boneless chuck, tip or round, cut into 1-inch cubes
¼    cup all-purpose flour
¼    cup vegetable oil
1    medium onion, chopped (about ½ cup)
2    slices bacon, cut up
1    can (15 ounces) garbanzo beans
4    tomatoes, chopped
¼    cup chopped carrot
¼    cup chopped celery
¾    cup tomato juice
¼    cup tequila
2    cloves garlic, finely chopped
2    tablespoons snipped cilantro
1½   teaspoons salt

Coat beef with flour. Heat oil in 10-inch skillet until hot. Cook and stir beef over medium heat until brown; remove beef and drain. Cook and stir onion and bacon in same skillet until bacon is crisp. Add beef and remaining ingredients. Heat to boiling; reduce heat. Cover and simmer until beef is tender, about 1 hour. *6 servings.*

# Spiced Sausage
## (Chorizos)

6    2-inch dried hot chilies
1½   teaspoons cumin seed
2    tablespoons vegetable oil
½    pound ground beef
½    pound ground pork
½    pound ground pork fat
¼    cup wine vinegar
¼    cup tequila
3    cloves garlic, finely chopped
1    tablespoon dried oregano leaves
1    tablespoon paprika
1    teaspoon salt
½    teaspoon ground cumin
¼    teaspoon sugar
¼    teaspoon pepper
⅛    teaspoon ground cloves
     Sausage casing*

Cook and stir chilies and cumin seed in oil until brown; drain and cool. Crush chilies. Mix chilies and remaining ingredients except sausage casing in glass or plastic bowl. Cover and refrigerate at least 24 hours to blend flavors.

Place mixture firmly in sausage casings; tie with string at 6-inch intervals. Place sausages on rack in refrigerator. Place waxed paper on rack below sausages. Refrigerate until dry, at least 1 day. Refrigerate no longer than 4 days. To cook, place sausages in cold skillet. Add 2 to 4 tablespoons water. Cover and cook slowly until done, about 8 minutes. Uncover and cook, turning sausages to brown evenly, until well done. *6 sausages.*

*Sausage casing can be omitted. The sausage mixture can be covered and refrigerated no longer than 4 days. Substitute ½ cup uncooked sausage mixture for each sausage removed from the casing. *3 cups sausage mixture.*

*Note:* Commerically prepared sausage can be substituted in recipes calling for sausage. Cook as directed above or as directed on the package.

# Peppers in Walnut Sauce
## (Chiles en Nogada)

8 poblano peppers
1 pound ground beef
1 small onion, chopped (about ¼ cup)
2 tomatoes, chopped
1 apple, chopped
1 banana, sliced
1 cup raisins
⅓ cup slivered almonds
2 tablespoons chopped olives
1 jalapeno pepper, seeded and finely chopped
1 clove garlic, finely chopped
1 tablespoon capers
½ teaspoon salt
¾ teaspoon ground cinnamon
¼ teaspoon cumin seed
¼ teaspoon ground oregano
⅛ teaspoon freshly ground pepper
4 eggs, separated
  Flour
  Vegetable oil
  Walnut Sauce (opposite)
  Pomegranate seeds or raisins
  Snipped cilantro

Set oven control to broil and/or 550°. Place poblano peppers on rack in broiler pan. (1) Broil peppers 4 to 5 inches from heat until skin blisters, about 5 minutes on each side. (2) Wrap in towels; let stand 5 minutes. (3) Peel peppers, starting at stem end. Cut a slit lengthwise down side of each pepper. Carefully remove seeds and membranes; rinse.

Cook and stir ground beef and onion in 10-inch skillet until beef is light brown; drain. Stir in remaining ingredients except eggs, flour, oil, Walnut Sauce, pomegranate seeds and cilantro. Cover and simmer 15 minutes. Fill peppers with stuffing. Cover and refrigerate 1 hour.

Beat egg whites until stiff. Beat egg yolks; fold into egg whites. Coat peppers with flour; dip into egg mixture. Heat ¼ inch oil until hot. Cook 1 pepper at a time, turning once, until puffy and golden, about 2 minutes on each side. Place on paper towels on cookie sheet; keep warm in 200° oven.

Prepare sauce; spoon sauce over each pepper. Sprinkle each with pomegranate seeds and cilantro. *8 servings.*

*Walnut Sauce:* Stir together 1 cup ground walnuts, 1 cup dairy sour cream and ½ cup Chicken Broth (page 26).

# Braised Meat Loaf
## (Albondigón de Carne)

1   pound ground beef
1   pound fully cooked smoked ham, finely chopped
1   pound ground pork
3   eggs
2   teaspoons salt
1/2   teaspoon pepper
1/4   teaspoon ground nutmeg
     Chipotle Sauce (opposite)
1/2   cup dry bread crumbs
1/4   cup masa harina
1/2   cup vegetable oil

Mix beef, ham, pork, eggs, salt, pepper and nutmeg; shape into loaf. Cover and refrigerate 1 hour. Prepare Chipotle Sauce. Mix bread crumbs and masa harina. Coat meat loaf with mixture.

Heat oil in 10-inch skillet until hot. Cook meat loaf in hot oil over medium heat until brown on all sides; drain. Pour sauce over meat loaf. Heat to boiling; reduce heat. Cover and simmer until done, about 1 hour. *12 servings.*

# Chili
## (Chile con Carne)

1   small onion, chopped (about 1/4 cup)
2   tablespoons chili powder
1   cup vegetable oil
1   cup water
1/4   cup tomato sauce
1   tablespoon cumin seed
1   tablespoon ground oregano
1   teaspoon salt
1   clove garlic, finely chopped
1   pound pork boneless shoulder,
        cut into 1/2-inch cubes
1/4   cup all-purpose flour
1   cup cooked Pinto Beans (page 79)
1   cup bean broth (page 79) or 1/2 cup water

Cook and stir onion and chili powder in 2 tablespoons of the oil in 1½-quart saucepan until onion is tender. Stir in water, tomato sauce, cumin, oregano, salt and garlic. Heat to boiling; reduce heat. Simmer uncovered 30 minutes.

Heat remaining oil in 10-inch skillet until hot. Coat pork with flour. Cook and stir pork until brown; drain on paper towels. Stir pork, beans and bean broth into sauce. Simmer uncovered until pork is tender, about 1 hour. *4 servings (about 1 cup each).*

*Chile con Carne II:* Substitute 1 pound ground beef for the pork. Omit water, flour and remaining oil. Cook and stir beef and onion until beef is brown; drain. Stir in remaining ingredients except beans and broth. Simmer uncovered 5 minutes. Stir in beans and broth; simmer 20 minutes.

# Meatballs in Chipotle Sauce
## (Albóndigas en Salsa de Chipotle)

     Chipotle Sauce (below)
1   pound ground beef
1   pound ground pork
1/2   cup dry bread crumbs
1/2   cup milk
2   tablespoons finely chopped onion
2   tablespoons snipped cilantro
2   teaspoons salt
1/2   teaspoon pepper
2   eggs

Prepare Chipotle Sauce. Mix remaining ingredients; shape into 1½-inch balls. Heat sauce and meatballs to boiling; reduce heat. Cover and simmer until meatballs are done, about 20 minutes. *8 servings.*

### Chipotle Sauce

2   to 4 dried chipotle peppers
2   slices bacon, finely cut up
1/4   cup finely chopped onion
4   tomatoes, finely chopped
1   cup Beef Broth (page 26)
1/4   cup finely chopped carrot
1/4   cup finely chopped celery
1/4   cup snipped cilantro
1/2   teaspoon salt
1/4   teaspoon pepper

Cover chipotle peppers with warm water. Let stand until tender, about 1 hour. Drain and chop finely. Cook and stir bacon and onion in oil in 2-quart saucepan until bacon is crisp; stir in peppers and remaining ingredients.

# Pork Marinade
## (Puerco Adobado)

2   *chipotle peppers*
6   *pork loin or rib chops, about ½ inch thick*
½   *cup orange juice concentrate*
¼   *cup vegetable oil*
    *Juice of 1 lemon (about ¼ cup)*
2   *tablespoons grated orange peel*
1   *clove garlic*
1   *teaspoon salt*
1   *medium orange, cut into 6 slices*

Cover chipotle peppers with warm water. Let stand until softened, about 1 hour. Place pork in shallow glass or plastic dish. Place peppers and remaining ingredients except orange in blender container. Cover and blend on low speed until smooth; pour over pork. Cover and refrigerate, spooning marinade over pork occasionally, at least 3 hours.

Set oven control to broil and/or 550°. Place pork on rack in broiler pan; place pan so top of pork is 3 to 5 inches from heat. Broil until light brown, about 10 minutes. Turn; brush with marinade and broil until pork is done, about 5 minutes. Garnish with orange slices. *6 servings.*

# Pork with Hominy and Greens
## (Puerco con Pozole)

¼   *cup vegetable oil*
6   *pork cubed steaks*
⅓   *cup all-purpose flour*
1   *medium onion, chopped (about ½ cup)*
1   *cup Beef Broth (page 26)*
1   *pound turnip or beet greens, coarsely chopped*
1   *can (20 ounces) hominy*
2   *tomatoes, chopped*
2   *slices bacon, cut up*
1   *tablespoon chili powder*
1   *tablespoon vinegar*
½   *teaspoon salt*
½   *teaspoon ground cumin*
½   *teaspoon ground oregano*
¼   *teaspoon pepper*

Heat oil in 4-quart Dutch oven until hot. Coat pork steaks with flour. Cook pork over medium heat until brown; drain on paper towels. Cook and stir onion in same skillet until tender. Stir in remaining ingredients; place pork on top. Heat to boiling; reduce heat. Cover and simmer until pork is tender, about 30 minutes. Garnish with snipped cilantro and chopped onion if desired. *6 servings.*

# Pork Chops in Radish Sauce
## (Chuletas de Puerco con Salsa de Rabanitos)

  Radish and Cilantro Relish (page 67)
2 tablespoons vegetable oil
6 pork loin or rib chops, about 1/2 inch thick
1 teaspoon salt
1/4 teaspoon pepper
2 tomatoes, chopped
  Hot cooked rice

Prepare Radish and Cilantro Relish. Heat oil in 10-inch skillet until hot. Cook pork over medium heat until brown; sprinkle with salt and pepper. Remove pork from skillet.

Cook and stir relish and tomatoes in same skillet 5 minutes. Add pork. Heat to boiling; reduce heat. Cover and simmer until pork is tender, about 45 minutes. Serve with rice. Garnish with snipped cilantro if desired. *6 servings.*

# Roast Loin of Pork
## (Asado de Puerco)

5 pound pork boneless top loin roast
  Juice of 2 limes (about 1/2 cup)
1/4 cup chili powder
1 can (6 ounces) frozen orange juice concentrate, thawed
2 cloves garlic, crushed
1 teaspoon salt
1 teaspoon ground cumin
1 teaspoon dried oregano leaves
1/2 teaspoon pepper
1/4 cup dry white wine
1/2 cup dairy sour cream
1/2 teaspoon salt

Place pork roast in shallow glass or plastic dish. Mix lime juice, chili powder, 1/4 cup of the concentrate, the garlic, 1 teaspoon salt, cumin, oregano and pepper. Brush mixture on pork. Cover and refrigerate at least 8 hours.

Place pork fat side up on rack in shallow roasting pan; insert meat thermometer so tip is in center of thickest part of pork and does not rest in fat. Roast uncovered in 325° oven until thermometer regis-

ters 170°, about 2 hours. Strain drippings from pan. Add enough water to remaining concentrate to measure 3/4 cup; stir juice and wine into drippings. Stir in sour cream and salt. Serve with pork. *12 to 15 servings.*

# Pork Tenderloin in Tequila
## (Lomo de Puerco al Tequila)

1/4 cup vegetable oil
2 cloves garlic, cut into halves
2 pounds pork tenderloin
1/4 cup prepared mustard
4 tomatoes, chopped
1 small onion, chopped (about 1/4 cup)
1/4 cup chopped carrot
1/4 cup chopped celery
  Juice of 1 lime (about 1/4 cup)
1/4 cup tequila
1 bay leaf
1 tablespoon chili powder
1 teaspoon salt
1 teaspoon dried oregano leaves
1 teaspoon dried thyme leaves
1/4 teaspoon pepper
1/4 cup snipped parsley

Heat oil and garlic in 10-inch skillet until hot. Coat pork with mustard. Cook pork over medium heat until brown. Remove garlic. Stir in remaining ingredients except parsley. Heat to boiling; reduce heat. Cover and simmer until pork is tender, about 30 minutes. Sprinkle with parsley. *6 servings.*

---

### ABOUT SOUR CREAM

When stirring sour cream into cooked vegetables or meat dishes, remove hot food from heat and gently fold or stir in sour cream just before serving. Overstirring or overheating can cause sour cream to thin and curdle. Curdling affects only the appearance, not the flavor of sour cream mixtures. Store dairy sour cream in original container in coldest part of refrigerator. Do not freeze since freezing causes cream to separate.

# Shredded Pork Tamales
## (Tamales de Puerco)

18   dried corn husks
 1   small onion, chopped (about ¼ cup)
 2   tablespoons vegetable oil
¼   cup Basic Red Sauce (page 65)
     Shredded Pork (right)
 2   tablespoons raisins
 2   tablespoons capers
 2   tablespoons snipped cilantro
     Tamale Dough (right)
18   pitted olives

Cover corn husks with warm water and let stand until pliable, at least 2 hours. Cook and stir onion in oil in 3-quart saucepan until tender. Stir in Red Sauce, Shredded Pork and remaining ingredients except Tamale Dough and olives. Heat to boiling; reduce heat. Cover and cook 15 minutes. (If mixture is too dry, add a little reserved pork liquid.) Prepare Tamale Dough.

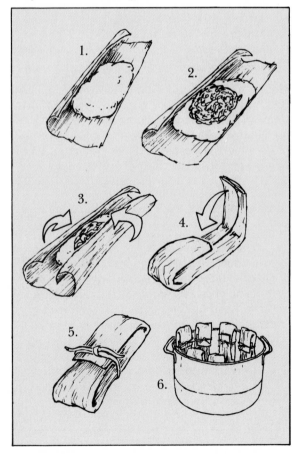

Drain corn husks; pat dry with paper towels. (1) Spread ¼ cup dough across center of each husk from 1 edge to within ½ inch of other edge. (2) Spoon 2 tablespoons pork mixture into center of dough; top with 1 olive. (3) Roll husks around filling starting with dough edge. (4) Fold both ends up toward center. (5) Secure with string if necessary. (6) Place tamales on rack in Dutch oven or steamer. Pour boiling water into Dutch oven to just under rack level. Cover Dutch oven. Keep water simmering over low heat 1 hour. *18 tamales.*

### Shredded Pork

 1   pound pork boneless shoulder
 1   tomato, chopped
 1   small onion, cut into fourths
 1   carrot, cut into 1-inch pieces
 1   stalk celery, cut into 1-inch pieces
 1   tablespoon chili powder
 1   teaspoon salt
¼   teaspoon cumin seed
¼   teaspoon dried oregano leaves
¼   teaspoon pepper
 1   clove garlic, crushed
 1   bay leaf

Place all ingredients in 3-quart saucepan. Add enough water to cover. Heat to boiling; reduce heat. Cover and simmer until pork is tender, about 1½ hours. Drain; reserve 2 cups broth for Tamale Dough. Cool and shred pork.

### Tamale Dough

 1   cup lard or shortening
 2   cups masa harina
 3   teaspoons baking powder
 1   teaspoon salt
 2   cups reserved pork broth

Beat all ingredients in large mixer bowl on low speed, scraping bowl constantly, until mixture forms a smooth paste. Beat on medium speed until light and fluffy, about 10 minutes.

# Pork in Green Sauce
## (Puerco en Salsa Verde)

2    pounds pork boneless shoulder, cut
       into 1-inch cubes
$\frac{1}{4}$   cup all-purpose flour
$\frac{1}{4}$   cup vegetable oil
1    medium onion, chopped (about $\frac{1}{2}$ cup)
1    can (13 ounces) tomatillos, drained and mashed
1    cup water
$\frac{1}{2}$   cup snipped cilantro
$\frac{1}{2}$   cup chopped green chilies
1    tablespoon dried oregano leaves
2    teaspoons instant chicken bouillon
1    teaspoon salt
$\frac{1}{4}$   teaspoon pepper
       Dairy sour cream

Coat pork with flour. Heat oil in 10-inch skillet until hot. Cook and stir pork over medium heat until brown; drain. Stir in remaining ingredients except sour cream. Heat to boiling; reduce heat. Cover and simmer until pork is tender, about 45 minutes. Garnish with sour cream; sprinkle with snipped cilantro if desired. *4 servings.*

# Pork and Cumin
## (Puerco al Comino)

2    pounds pork boneless shoulder, cut
       into 1-inch cubes
$\frac{1}{4}$   cup all-purpose flour
$\frac{1}{2}$   cup vegetable oil
1    medium onion, chopped (about $\frac{1}{2}$ cup)
2    slices bacon, cut up
$\frac{1}{2}$   cup water
4    tomatoes, chopped
2    medium potatoes, diced
2    tablespoons orange juice
       Juice of $\frac{1}{2}$ lime (about 2 tablespoons)
2    teaspoons instant chicken bouillon
2    teaspoons cumin seed
1    teaspoon dried oregano leaves
$\frac{1}{2}$   teaspoon salt
$\frac{1}{4}$   teaspoon pepper
$\frac{1}{2}$   cup dairy sour cream

Coat pork with flour. Heat oil in 10-inch skillet until hot. Cook and stir pork over medium heat until brown; drain. Cook and stir onion and bacon in same skillet until bacon is crisp. Stir in pork and remaining ingredients except sour cream. Heat to boiling; reduce heat. Cover and simmer until pork is tender, about 45 minutes. Stir in sour cream; heat until hot. *7 servings.*

# Salads, Relishes & Sauces

## Chicken and Orange Salad
### (Ensalada de Pollo con Naranja)

| | |
|---|---|
| 2 | tablespoons finely chopped scallions or green onions (with tops) |
| | Juice of ½ lime (about 2 tablespoons) |
| 1 | teaspoon salt |
| 2 | cups cut-up cooked chicken |
| 1 | cup cooked green peas |
| ¼ | cup finely chopped carrots |
| ¼ | cup finely chopped celery |
| ¼ | cup finely chopped cilantro |
| 1 | cup mayonnaise or salad dressing |
| | Juice of ½ orange (about 3 tablespoons) |
| 1 | teaspoon salt |
| ½ | teaspoon ground cinnamon |
| ¼ | teaspoon freshly ground pepper |
| | Lettuce leaves |
| 3 | oranges, pared and sectioned |
| 2 | avocados, cut into wedges |

Sprinkle scallions with lime juice and 1 teaspoon salt. Cover and refrigerate. Mix remaining ingredients except lettuce, oranges and avocados; cover and refrigerate at least 1 hour. Spoon salad on lettuce. Garnish with oranges and avocados; sprinkle with scallions. *6 servings.*

## Shrimp and Potato Salad
### (Ensalada de Papa y Camarón)

| | |
|---|---|
| 2½ | cups cooked small shrimp |
| 2 | cups cubed cooked potatoes |
| 1 | cup cooked green peas |
| ¼ | cup chopped celery |
| | Juice of ½ lime (about 2 tablespoons) |
| 1 | teaspoon ground cumin |
| ¼ | teaspoon salt |
| ⅛ | teaspoon freshly ground pepper |
| ¾ | cup mayonnaise or salad dressing |
| ¼ | cup snipped cilantro (reserve 1 tablespoon) |
| | Lettuce leaves |
| 3 | tomatoes, cut into wedges |

Mix shrimp, potatoes, peas, celery, lime juice, cumin, salt and pepper. Cover and refrigerate at least 2 hours. Just before serving, toss with mayonnaise and 3 tablespoons cilantro until potatoes are well coated. Serve on lettuce; garnish with tomatoes and reserved cilantro. *6 servings.*

*Chicken and Orange Salad*

## Mexican Chicken Salad
(Ensalada de Pollo a la Mexicana)

2    cups cut-up cooked chicken
1/4   cup dairy sour cream
1/4   cup mayonnaise or salad dressing
1    small onion, chopped (about 1/4 cup)
1/4   cup finely chopped carrot
2    tablespoons snipped cilantro
     Juice of 1/2 lime (about 2 tablespoons)
2    tablespoons capers
2    tablespoons chopped pimiento
1/2   teaspoon ground cumin
1/2   teaspoon dried oregano leaves
     Lettuce leaves
1    avocado, cut into wedges
     Paprika

Toss all ingredients except lettuce, avocado and paprika. Serve salad on lettuce. Garnish with avocado; sprinkle with paprika. *4 servings.*

## Tossed Romaine Salad
(Ensalada de Romanita)

1    clove garlic, cut into halves
2    anchovy fillets
1/4   cup olive or vegetable oil
1/4   cup grated Parmesan cheese
1    tablespoon lime juice
1    teaspoon Worcestershire sauce
1    teaspoon salt
1/8   teaspoon freshly ground pepper
1    large or 2 small bunches romaine, torn into
       bite-size pieces (about 8 cups)
1    cup croutons

Rub large wooden salad bowl with cut clove of garlic. Mash anchovies with fork in salad bowl. Stir in oil, cheese, lime juice, Worcestershire sauce, salt and pepper. Add romaine and croutons; toss until leaves glisten. *6 servings.*

## Spinach and Mushroom Salad
(Ensalada Leopoldina)

Mix 4 ounces mushrooms, sliced, and 1/4 cup Herbed Vinaigrette (page 21). Cover and refrigerate at least 30 minutes. Just before serving, toss mushrooms with 8 ounces spinach, torn into bite-size pieces. *8 servings.*

## Cactus Salad
(Ensalada de Nopalitos)

1    medium onion, thinly sliced
1/2   cup Herbed Vinaigrette (page 21)
1    can (26 ounces) chopped cactus, drained
1/4   cup chopped pimiento
     Lettuce

Mix onion and Herbed Vinaigrette in glass or plastic bowl. Cover and refrigerate at least 1 hour. Toss onion mixture with cactus and pimiento. Serve on lettuce. *6 servings.*

## Orange Salad with Pecan Dressing
(Ensalada de Naranja con Salsa de Nuez)

4    oranges
1    head lettuce, torn into bite-size pieces
1/4   cup ground pecans
2    tablespoons mayonnaise or salad dressing
2    tablespoons dairy sour cream
1    tablespoon lime juice
1/2   teaspoon sugar
1/2   teaspoon salt
1/8   teaspoon ground cinnamon
     Dash of pepper

Pare and slice oranges; cut slices into fourths. Mix oranges and lettuce. Mix remaining ingredients; pour over oranges and lettuce and toss. *6 servings.*

*Cauliflower and Avocado Salad and Savory Summer Salad*

# Cauliflower and Avocado Salad
## (Ensalada de Coliflor)

1   medium cauliflower, separated into flowerets
2   tablespoons vinegar
2   tablespoons vegetable oil
½   teaspoon salt
    Dash of pepper
    Romaine
    Avocado Dip (page 17)
2   tablespoons slivered almonds

Heat 1 inch water to boiling. Add cauliflower; cover and heat to boiling. Cook 4 minutes; drain. Immediately rinse under running cold water; drain. Mix vinegar and oil in large glass or plastic bowl. Add cauliflower, salt and pepper; toss. Cover and refrigerate at least 1 hour.

Just before serving, arrange cauliflower on romaine; top with Avocado Dip. Sprinkle with almonds. *6 to 8 servings.*

# Savory Summer Salad
## (Ensalada Mixta)

4   scallions or green onions (with tops),
        finely chopped
¼   cup vegetable oil
    Juice of ½ lime (about 2 tablespoons)
1   clove garlic, finely chopped
1   teaspoon dried oregano leaves
¼   to ½ teaspoon finely crushed dried chipotle pepper
¼   teaspoon salt
    Dash of pepper
2   oranges, pared and sectioned
1   cucumber, thinly sliced
    Lettuce

Mix scallions, oil, lime juice, garlic, oregano, chipotle pepper, salt and pepper in glass or plastic bowl. Cover and refrigerate at least 1 hour. Toss scallion mixture, oranges and cucumber. Serve on lettuce. *6 servings.*

# Pinto Bean Salad
## (Ensalada de Frijoles)

2 cups Pinto Beans (page 79)
1 cup finely chopped celery
¼ cup finely chopped onion
¼ cup snipped parsley
1 clove garlic, finely chopped
1 tablespoon ground cumin
½ teaspoon salt
⅛ teaspoon freshly ground pepper
¼ cup mayonnaise or salad dressing
¼ cup vegetable oil
  Juice of ½ lime (about 2 tablespoons)

Toss all ingredients. Cover and refrigerate until chilled, about 2 hours. *6 servings.*

# Festive Tricolor Salad
## (Ensalada Tricolor II)

2 large potatoes, cut into ½-inch pieces
4 tomatoes, cut into wedges
1 ripe avocado, cut into wedges
  Avocado and Raisin Dressing (below) or
    Herbed Vinaigrette (page 21)

Heat 1 inch water to boiling. Add potatoes; cover and heat to boiling. Cook 5 minutes; drain. Immediately rinse under running cold water; drain. Toss potatoes, tomatoes and avocado with dressing. *6 to 8 servings.*

### Avocado and Raisin Dressing

1 avocado, cut up
½ cup vegetable oil
¼ cup raisins
¼ cup orange juice
¼ cup dairy sour cream
1 tablespoon lime juice
½ teaspoon sugar
¼ teaspoon salt
⅛ teaspoon freshly ground pepper
2 tablespoons snipped cilantro

Place all ingredients except cilantro in blender container. Cover and blend on high speed until smooth. Stir in cilantro. *1½ cups.*

# Mexican Flag Salad
## (Ensalada Tricolor I)

6 cups water
  Juice of ½ lime (about 2 tablespoons)
16 ounces whole green beans
1 small jicama, cut into julienne strips
    (about 2 cups)
2 red peppers, seeded and cut into julienne strips
  Herbed Vinaigrette (page 21)
1 teaspoon chili powder
  Lettuce leaves
6 to 8 ripe olives, finely chopped

Heat water and lime juice to boiling. Place beans in wire strainer; lower into boiling water. Cover and cook 5 minutes. Immediately rinse under running cold water; drain.

Place beans, jicama and red peppers in individual bowls. Mix Herbed Vinaigrette and chili powder. Pour ¼ cup of the vinaigrette mixture over each vegetable. Cover and refrigerate at least 1 hour.

Arrange beans, jicama and red peppers on lettuce leaves in Mexican flag design. Place olives in center of rectangle formed by jicama. *6 to 8 servings.*

### ABOUT MEXICAN FLAG SALAD

The national colors of Mexico are green, white and red. The green symbolizes the lofty hopes of the new Republic; the white stands for the purity of its endeavors and the red for the valor displayed in pursuit of these noble goals. The Mexican Flag Salad represents these colors with green, white and red vegetables and the chopped ripe olives simulate the black eagle on the flag.

*Mexican Flag Salad*

# Basic Green Sauce
## (Salsa Verde)

 2  medium onions, chopped (about 1 cup)
½  cup vegetable oil
10  ounces spinach, chopped
 1  can (13 ounces) whole green Spanish tomatoes
 1  can (4 ounces) chopped green chilies
 2  cloves garlic, crushed
 1  tablespoon dried oregano leaves
 1  cup Chicken Broth (page 26)

Cook and stir onions in oil in 3-quart saucepan until tender. Add spinach, tomatoes (with liquid), green chilies (with liquid), garlic and oregano. Cover and cook over medium heat 5 minutes. Transfer to blender container; cover and blend on low speed until smooth, about 1 minute.

Return mixture to saucepan; stir in Chicken Broth. Heat to boiling; reduce heat. Simmer uncovered 10 minutes. Cover and refrigerate sauce no longer than 10 days. *About 4½ cups sauce.*

*Note:* A bottled mild green chili sauce can be substituted in recipes calling for Basic Green Sauce. The flavor is the same but the purchased sauce may be red rather than green. A bottled green taco sauce can be substituted but the flavor is hotter.

# Basic Red Sauce
## (Salsa de Chile Rojo)

| | |
|---|---|
| 8 | chile anchos* |
| 3½ | cups warm water |
| 1 | medium onion, chopped |
| 2 | cloves garlic, chopped |
| ¼ | cup vegetable oil |
| 1 | can (8 ounces) tomato sauce |
| 1 | tablespoon dried oregano leaves |
| 1 | tablespoon cumin seed |
| 1 | teaspoon salt |

Soak chilies in water until softened, about 30 minutes. Drain; strain and reserve liquid. Remove stems, seeds and membranes from chilies. Cook and stir onion and garlic in oil in 2-quart saucepan until onion is tender. Add chilies and 2 cups of the reserved liquid, the tomato sauce, oregano, cumin and salt. Simmer uncovered 20 minutes. Cool.

Transfer to blender container; cover and blend on low speed until smooth. Strain. Refrigerate sauce no longer than 10 days. *About 2½ cups sauce.*

*2 cups chicken broth and ¼ cup chili powder can be substituted for chile anchos and water.

*Note:* A canned red chili puree or mild red taco sauce can be substituted in recipes calling for Basic Red Sauce.

# Casera Sauce
## (Salsa Casera)

| | |
|---|---|
| 2 | medium tomatoes, finely chopped |
| 1 | medium onion, chopped (about ½ cup) |
| 1 | small clove garlic, finely chopped |
| 1 | canned jalapeno pepper, seeded and finely chopped |
| 1 | tablespoon finely snipped cilantro |
| 1 | tablespoon lemon juice |
| 1½ | teaspoons vegetable oil |
| ½ | teaspoon dried oregano leaves |
| ½ | teaspoon jalapeno pepper liquid |

Mix all ingredients. Cover and refrigerate in glass or plastic container. Refrigerate no longer than 7 days. *About 2 cups sauce.*

*Note:* A bottled tomato and yellow chili sauce can be substituted in recipes calling for Casera Sauce.

*Hot Pickled Vegetables*

# Hot Pickled Vegetables
## (Curados)

|   |   |
|---|---|
| 2 | cups cider vinegar |
| 2 | cups water |
| 1½ | cups cauliflower flowerets |
| 3 | stalks celery, cut into julienne strips (about 1½ cups) |
| 2 | medium carrots, cut diagonally into thin slices (about 1 cup) |
| 1 | cup broccoli flowerets |
| 4 | ounces whole green beans |
| ½ | cup fresh or canned serrano peppers or jalapeno pepper slices |
| 1 | cup pearl onions |
| ½ | cup coarse salt |
| 2 | tablespoons peppercorns |
| ¾ | teaspoon ground cloves |

Mix all ingredients in large glass container. Cover and refrigerate at least 48 hours. Store no longer than 2 weeks. *About 10 cups.*

## ABOUT CHILIES

Perhaps the most characteristic ingredient in Mexican cooking is the chili, a kind of pepper used both as a seasoning and as a vegetable. All peppers grown in the Western hemisphere are members of the capsicum family. They include bell peppers, pimientos and chilies, all rich sources of Vitamins A and C.

There are many varieties of chilies, which range in flavor from fiery hot to sweet and mild. The degree of hotness is determined by a substance in the veins called capsaicin. The seeds of chilies do contribute to the high level of seasoning because of their close contact with the veins. For a milder chili flavor, remove both veins and seeds from chilies.

*Warning:* wear rubber gloves when handling hot chilies because capsaicin can cause severe irritation if it comes in contact with skin or eyes. Wash hands with soap and warm water after handling chilies.

## Zucchini with Lime and Cilantro
(Calabacitas con Limón y Cilantro)

2   cups shredded zucchini
1/4  cup chopped cilantro
    Juice of 1/2 lime (about 2 tablespoons)
2   tablespoons olive or vegetable oil
1   teaspoon salt
1/4  teaspoon sugar
1/4  teaspoon pepper

Mix all ingredients in glass or plastic bowl. Cover and refrigerate at least 1 hour. Serve on lettuce leaves if desired. *1 1/4 cups.*

## Radish and Cilantro Relish
(Salsa de Rabanitos y Cilantro)

2   cups thinly sliced radishes (about 24 radishes)
1   medium onion, chopped (about 1/2 cup)
    Juice of 1/2 orange (about 3 tablespoons)
    Juice of 1 lime (about 2 tablespoons)
2   tablespoons finely snipped cilantro
2   tablespoons vegetable oil
1/4  teaspoon salt
1/8  teaspoon freshly ground pepper

Mix all ingredients in glass or plastic bowl. Cover and refrigerate at least 1 hour. Serve on salad greens if desired. *6 servings.*

# Vegetables, Rice & Beans

## Vegetable Pears
### (Chayotes)

4 chayotes
2 slices bacon, cut into ½-inch pieces
4 tomatoes, chopped
1 large onion, chopped (about 1 cup)
1 clove garlic, finely chopped
2 tablespoons vegetable oil
½ teaspoon salt
½ teaspoon dried oregano leaves
¼ teaspoon ground nutmeg
¼ teaspoon pepper
1 cup shredded cheese (about 4 ounces)

Peel chayotes; cut lengthwise into fourths. Remove seeds and fibers; discard fibers. Heat enough salted water to cover chayotes (½ teaspoon salt to 1 cup water) to boiling. Add chayotes and seeds. Cover and cook until chayotes are crisp-tender, 15 to 20 minutes; drain.

Cook and stir bacon in 2-quart saucepan until crisp. Add tomatoes, onion, garlic, oil, salt, oregano, nutmeg and pepper. Heat to boiling; reduce heat. Simmer uncovered 15 minutes. Arrange chayotes in ungreased rectangular baking dish, 13 × 9 × 2 inches. Pour sauce over chayotes; sprinkle with cheese. Cook uncovered in 350° oven until hot and bubbly and cheese is melted, about 15 minutes. *8 servings.*

## Mustard Artichoke Hearts
### (Corazones de Alcachofa a la Mostaza)

1 small onion, chopped (about ¼ cup)
2 tablespoons margarine or butter
2 tablespoons brandy
1 clove garlic, finely chopped
1 tablespoon prepared mustard
½ teaspoon ground cumin
½ teaspoon salt
⅛ teaspoon pepper
2 cans (14 ounces each) artichoke hearts*, drained and cut into halves
¼ cup snipped parsley

Cook and stir onion in margarine in 10-inch skillet over medium heat until tender. Add brandy; simmer uncovered 2 minutes. Stir in garlic, mustard, cumin, salt and pepper; add artichokes. Simmer uncovered, stirring occasionally, 5 minutes. Stir in parsley. *6 servings.*

*2 packages (9 ounces each) frozen artichoke hearts can be substituted for the canned. Cook as directed on package.

*Vegetable Pears*

*Carrots with Green Grapes*

## Carrots with Green Grapes
### (Zanahorias con Uvas)

8   medium carrots
2   tablespoons margarine or butter
1   tablespoon sugar
1   teaspoon salt
2   cups seedless green grapes
¼   teaspoon dried tarragon leaves
½   cup dairy sour cream
2   tablespoons water

Cut carrots crosswise into halves. Cut each half lengthwise into ½-inch strips. Heat 1 inch salted water (½ teaspoon salt to 1 cup water) to boiling. Add carrots. Cover and cook until crisp-tender, about 5 minutes; drain.

Melt margarine in 10-inch skillet over medium-high heat. Add carrots, sugar and salt; cook and stir 5 minutes. Stir in grapes and tarragon; heat until hot. Remove from heat; stir in sour cream and water. *6 servings.*

## Eggplant Fritters
### (Frituras de Berenjena)

    Vegetable oil
1   medium eggplant, pared and shredded
        (about 2½ cups)
1   egg
1   cup all-purpose flour
1   teaspoon salt
½   teaspoon baking powder
¼   teaspoon ground nutmeg
⅛   teaspoon pepper
2   scallions or green onions (with tops),
        finely chopped

Heat vegetable oil (2 inches) to 375°. Mix eggplant, egg, flour, salt, baking powder, nutmeg and pepper. Drop by rounded teaspoonfuls into hot oil. Fry until golden brown, turning once, about 2 minutes. Drain on paper towels; sprinkle with scallions. *About 2 dozen fritters.*

# Eggplant with Cheese
## (Berenjena con Queso)

1   large eggplant
1   teaspoon salt
½   cup vegetable oil
1   cup ricotta cheese
1   cup shredded Cheddar cheese (about 4 ounces)
¼   cup grated Parmesan cheese

Pare eggplant; cut into ¼-inch slices. Cut each slice into 2-inch pieces. Sprinkle with salt; let stand 30 minutes. Drain eggplant and pat dry. Cook eggplant, turning occasionally, in oil until light golden brown; drain on paper towels.

Mix ricotta and Cheddar cheese; place 1 rounded teaspoon cheese mixture on one end of each eggplant slice. Roll up from cheese end. Place on rack in broiler pan; sprinkle with Parmesan cheese. Set oven control to broil and/or 550°. Broil with tops 3 to 4 inches from heat until golden brown, about 5 minutes. *4 or 5 servings.*

---

## ABOUT CHEESE

Cheese became a distinctive ingredient in Mexican cooking with the introduction of cows and goats by the Spaniards. Many varieties, which contribute taste and texture to Mexican dishes, are used for stuffing, layering and topping in recipes.

Store cheese in refrigerator. Wrap it tightly in aluminum foil or plastic wrap to prevent moisture loss. Firm cheeses such as Cheddar keep two months or more; semisoft cheeses such as Monterey Jack keep about 3 weeks and soft cheeses such as cream cheese, about 2 weeks. If mold forms on cheese other than Roquefort and blue cheeses, which are mold-ripened, cut it off. If mold has penetrated cheese, discard the cheese. Freeze slices and pieces of cheese tightly wrapped in moisture-proof freezer wrap for up to 3 months. Thaw in refrigerator rather than at room temperature to prevent excessive crumbling.

# Stewed Eggplant
## (Berenjenas Sancochadas)

2   medium eggplants
1   tablespoon coarse salt
½   cup all-purpose flour
½   cup vegetable oil
1   medium onion, chopped (about ½ cup)
2   tomatoes, chopped
    Juice of ½ lime (about 2 tablespoons)
1   clove garlic, finely chopped
1   teaspoon dried oregano leaves
½   teaspoon salt
¼   teaspoon pepper

Cut each eggplant crosswise into halves; cut each half lengthwise into ½-inch strips. Sprinkle eggplant with salt; let stand 15 minutes. Pat eggplant dry with paper towels. Toss eggplant with flour until evenly coated.

Heat oil in 10-inch skillet over medium-high heat until hot. Cook about ⅓ of the eggplant, turning once, until brown and crisp, about 4 minutes. Drain on paper towels. Repeat with remaining eggplant. Cook and stir onion in same skillet over medium heat until tender. Add remaining ingredients; simmer uncovered, stirring occasionally, 10 minutes. Stir in eggplant; heat until hot. *6 to 8 servings.*

# Wilted Spinach
## (Espinaca en Mantequilla)

1   medium onion, chopped (about ½ cup)
1   slice bacon, cut up
1   clove garlic, finely chopped
2   tablespoons margarine or butter
2   tablespoons olive or vegetable oil
½   teaspoon salt
¼   teaspoon pepper
¼   teaspoon ground nutmeg
16  ounces spinach
    Juice of ½ lime (about 2 tablespoons)

Cook and stir onion, bacon and garlic in margarine and oil in 4-quart Dutch oven over medium heat until bacon is crisp. Reduce heat; stir in salt, pepper and nutmeg. Add spinach; toss just until spinach is wilted. Drizzle with lime juice. *6 servings.*

# Sautéed Green and Red Peppers
## (Chiles en Crema)

2   slices bacon, cut up
2   tablespoons margarine or butter
2   green peppers, cut into ¼-inch strips
2   red peppers, cut into ¼-inch strips
1   small onion, chopped (about ¼ cup)
2   tomatoes, chopped
1   teaspoon cumin seed
1   teaspoon dried oregano leaves
1   teaspoon salt
¼   teaspoon pepper
½   cup dairy sour cream
    Snipped cilantro

Cook and stir bacon in margarine in 10-inch skillet until crisp; remove and drain on paper towels. Cook and stir green and red peppers and onion in same skillet over medium-high heat 2 minutes. Add remaining ingredients except sour cream and cilantro. Heat to boiling; reduce heat and simmer uncovered 5 minutes. Remove from heat and stir in sour cream; sprinkle with cilantro. *6 servings.*

# Mexican Succotash
## (Calabacitas a la Mexicana)

3   medium zucchini
2   ears fresh corn*
1   medium onion, chopped (about ½ cup)
¼   cup vegetable oil
1   can (28 ounces) Italian plum tomatoes
1   teaspoon salt
1   teaspoon dried oregano leaves
    Dash of pepper

Cut zucchini into ½-inch slices. Cut kernels from corn. Cook and stir onion in oil in 10-inch skillet over medium heat until tender. Add zucchini; cook and stir 1 minute. Stir in corn and remaining ingredients. Heat to boiling; reduce heat. Cover and simmer until zucchini is tender, about 15 minutes. *6 servings.*

*1 package (10 ounces) frozen corn can be substituted for the fresh corn.

# Mashed Carrots and Potatoes
## (Puré de Zanahoria y Papa)

2   cups Chicken Broth (page 26) or water
4   medium carrots, cut into ½-inch slices
2   medium potatoes, cut into 1-inch pieces
½   cup half-and-half
1   tablespoon margarine or butter
1   teaspoon cumin seed
1   teaspoon ground cinnamon
¼   teaspoon ground nutmeg

Heat Chicken Broth to boiling. Add carrots and potatoes. Cover and heat to boiling. Cook until carrots are tender, 18 to 20 minutes; drain. Mash carrots and potatoes until no lumps remain. Stir in remaining ingredients. *4 servings.*

*Mexican Succotash and
Sautéed Green and Red Peppers*

# Cauliflower with Avocado-Almond Sauce
## (Coliflor con Salsa de Aguacate y Almendro)

1   medium cauliflower
    Herbed Vinaigrette (page 21)
1   ripe avocado
    Juice of ½ lemon (about 2 tablespoons)
¼   cup snipped cilantro
1   teaspoon ground cumin
½   teaspoon salt
¼   teaspoon sugar
¼   teaspoon pepper
¼   cup ground toasted almonds

Heat 1 inch salted water (½ teaspoon salt to 1 cup water) to boiling. Add whole cauliflower. Cover and heat to boiling. Cook until crisp-tender, 8 to 10 minutes. Pour Herbed Vinaigrette over cauliflower in glass or plastic bowl. Cover and refrigerate at least 1 hour.

Mash avocado with fork until smooth. Stir in remaining ingredients except almonds. Spread cauliflower with avocado mixture; sprinkle with almonds. Cut into wedges to serve. *6 servings.*

# Cauliflower-Cheese Bake
## (Coliflor con Queso)

1   medium cauliflower, separated into flowerets
1   medium onion, chopped (about ½ cup)
2   tablespoons vegetable oil
1   green pepper, chopped
1   tomato, chopped
1   jalapeno pepper, seeded and finely chopped
1   tablespoon coarsely chopped green olives
1   tablespoon snipped parsley
1   teaspoon salt
1   teaspoon capers
1   clove garlic, finely chopped
¼   cup dry bread crumbs
½   cup shredded Cheddar cheese

Heat 1 inch salted water (½ teaspoon salt to 1 cup water) to boiling. Add cauliflower. Cover and cook 5 minutes; drain. Arrange cauliflower in ungreased baking dish, 10 × 6 × 1½ inches.

Cook and stir onion in oil in 10-inch skillet until tender. Add green pepper, tomato, jalapeno pepper, olives, parsley, salt, capers and garlic; simmer uncovered 5 minutes. Pour over cauliflower. Sprinkle with bread crumbs and cheese. Cook uncovered in 350° oven until cheese is melted, about 15 minutes. *5 servings.*

---

## ABOUT KEEPING FOOD SAFE

When you shop for groceries, plan to pick up perishable foods last. Refrigerate or freeze them as soon as possible after purchase. Use fresh meats within 3 days and variety meats (such as honeycomb tripe) within 24 hours. Use fresh fish and poultry within 2 days; freeze for longer storage. Keep frozen food at 0°F. Eggs, fish and meat should always be cooked rather than eaten raw.

Do not allow hot or cold foods to remain at room temperature for more than 2 hours; bacteria thrive in lukewarm foods and may not be detected because they seldom change the taste, odor or appearance of food. A standard rule, recommended by the U.S. Department of Agriculture, is that hot foods should be kept hot (about 140°) and cold foods cold (below 40°). Once food has been cooked, keep it hot until serving time or refrigerate as soon as possible.

### Safe Buffet Service

Serve food in small dishes, refilling frequently from stove or refrigerator; or keep foods hot in electric frypans or chafing dishes or on hot trays. Do not depend on warming units that use small candles.

Refrigerate recipes made with eggs, milk or cream and all salads or dips made with mayonnaise, seafood, poultry or meat. Ideally, chill both food and dish before serving. Serve cold foods over crushed ice to keep them cold.

## Stewed Mexican Vegetables
## (Cocido de Vegetales)

1 medium onion, chopped (about ½ cup)
2 tablespoons margarine or butter
2 tablespoons vegetable oil
1 medium zucchini, chopped
4 tomatoes, chopped
¼ cup snipped parsley
2 tablespoons chili powder
¼ teaspoon ground nutmeg
¼ teaspoon ground cinnamon
  Corn Batter (below)

Cook and stir onion in margarine and oil in 10-inch skillet until tender. Stir in remaining ingredients except Corn Batter. Heat to boiling; reduce heat. Simmer uncovered 10 minutes. Prepare Corn Batter; drop by rounded teaspoonfuls onto hot sauce. Cook uncovered over low heat 10 minutes. Cover and cook 10 minutes longer. *10 servings.*

### Corn Batter

1 can (8¾ ounces) whole kernel corn, drained
¼ cup milk
¼ cup chopped pimiento
¼ teaspoon salt
  Dash of pepper
½ cup all-purpose flour
½ cup shredded cheese (about 2 ounces)
½ teaspoon baking powder
1 egg, separated

Mix all ingredients except egg white. Beat egg white in small mixer bowl until stiff but not dry. Fold corn mixture into egg white.

## Corn Soufflé
## (Soufflé de Elote)

3 tablespoons margarine or butter
3 tablespoons all-purpose flour
¼ teaspoon sugar
¼ teaspoon ground cumin
¼ teaspoon ground nutmeg
¼ teaspoon ground red pepper
1 cup milk
3 egg yolks, slightly beaten
1 can (8¾ ounces) whole kernel corn, drained
2 tablespoons finely chopped onion
2 tablespoons finely chopped green chilies
3 egg whites
  Chile with Cheese Sauce (below)

Heat oven to 350°. Butter 5-cup soufflé dish or 1-quart casserole. Heat margarine over low heat until melted. Stir in flour, sugar, cumin, nutmeg and red pepper. Cook over low heat, stirring constantly, until mixture is smooth and bubbly. Stir in milk; heat to boiling, stirring constantly. Boil and stir 1 minute. Stir at least half of the hot mixture gradually into egg yolks. Blend into hot mixture in saucepan. Boil and stir 1 minute; remove from heat. Stir in corn, onion and green chilies.

Beat egg whites in small mixer bowl until stiff. Stir about ¼ of the egg whites into corn mixture. Fold corn mixture into remaining egg whites. Carefully pour into soufflé dish. Cook uncovered until knife inserted halfway between center and edge comes out clean, about 50 minutes. Serve immediately with Sauce. *6 servings.*

### Chile with Cheese Sauce

½ cup shredded cheese (about 2 ounces)
⅓ cup half-and-half
¼ cup finely chopped green chilies
1 tablespoon finely chopped onion
1 teaspoon ground cumin
¼ teaspoon salt

Heat all ingredients over low heat, stirring constantly, until cheese is melted.

# Sautéed Mushrooms
## (Hongos en Mantequilla)

2   *slices buttered toast*
1   *small onion, chopped (about ¼ cup)*
2   *tablespoons margarine or butter*
2   *tablespoons olive or vegetable oil*
16  *ounces mushrooms, sliced*
   *Juice of 1 lemon (about ¼ cup)*
1   *clove garlic, finely chopped*
1   *teaspoon ground nutmeg*
½  *teaspoon salt*
   *Dash of pepper*
¼  *cup snipped parsley*

Remove crusts from toast. Cut each slice into 4 triangles. Cook and stir onion in margarine and oil in 10-inch skillet over medium heat until tender. Add remaining ingredients except toast and parsley; reduce heat and simmer uncovered 5 minutes. Stir in parsley; serve over toast triangles. *4 servings.*

---

# Green Beans
## (Ejotes)

1   *pound green beans*
4   *slices bacon, cut up*
1   *medium onion, chopped (about ½ cup)*
1   *tomato, chopped*
1   *clove garlic, finely chopped*
½  *teaspoon dried oregano leaves*
½  *teaspoon salt*
   *Dash of pepper*
   *Juice of ½ lemon (about 2 tablespoons)*

Heat beans and 1 inch salted water (½ teaspoon salt to 1 cup water) to boiling. Cook uncovered 5 minutes. Cover and cook until tender, 5 to 10 minutes. Immediately rinse under cold water; drain.

Fry bacon in 10-inch skillet until crisp; drain on paper towels. Cook and stir onion in bacon fat until tender. Add tomato, garlic, oregano, salt and pepper; simmer uncovered 5 minutes. Stir in beans; heat until hot. Drizzle with lemon juice and garnish with bacon. *4 servings.*

---

# Baked Stuffed Tomatoes
## (Tomates Rellenos)

6   *large tomatoes*
1   *medium onion, chopped (about ½ cup)*
1   *clove garlic, finely chopped*
2   *tablespoons margarine or butter*
⅓  *cup white wine*
1   *cup chopped fully cooked smoked ham*
½  *cup dry bread crumbs*
¼  *cup snipped parsley*
2   *anchovy fillets, finely chopped*
   *Juice of ½ lime (about 2 tablespoons)*
1   *teaspoon dried oregano leaves*
1   *teaspoon dried basil leaves*
¼  *teaspoon salt*
⅛  *teaspoon pepper*
⅓  *cup shredded cheese (about 1½ ounces)*

Remove stem ends from tomatoes; cut thin slice from bottom of each tomato to prevent tipping. Remove pulp, leaving a ½-inch wall; chop enough pulp to measure ½ cup.

Cook and stir onion and garlic in margarine in 10-inch skillet over medium heat until onion is tender. Add wine; simmer uncovered 3 minutes. Stir in tomato pulp and remaining ingredients except cheese. Place tomatoes in ungreased rectangular baking dish, 10 × 6 × 1½ inches. Fill tomatoes with ham mixture; sprinkle with cheese. Cook uncovered in 350° oven until tomatoes are heated through, about 20 minutes. Garnish with sour cream and fresh snipped basil or parsley if desired. *6 servings.*

---

*Top to bottom: Baked Stuffed Tomatoes, Sautéed Mushrooms and Green Beans*

# Zucchini and Hominy
## (Calabacitas con Pozole)

1   small onion, chopped (about ¼ cup)
2   tablespoons margarine or butter
2   tablespoons vegetable oil
3   medium zucchini, cut into ½-inch pieces
1   can (20 ounces) hominy, drained
2   tomatoes, chopped
    Juice of ½ lime (about 2 tablespoons)
1   tablespoon chili powder
1   teaspoon salt
    Dash of pepper

Cook and stir onion in margarine and oil in 10-inch skillet over medium heat until tender. Stir in remaining ingredients; cook uncovered, stirring ocassionally, until zucchini is tender, 10 to 15 minutes. *5 or 6 servings.*

# Mexican Rice
## (Arroz a la Mexicana)

1   clove garlic, cut into halves
2   tablespoons vegetable oil
1   cup uncooked long grain rice
2   cups Chicken Broth (page 26)
¼   cup Casera Sauce (page 65)

Cook and stir garlic in oil in 2-quart saucepan over medium heat until brown; remove garlic. Cook and stir rice in oil until golden, about 5 minutes. Stir in Chicken Broth and Casera Sauce. Heat to boiling, stirring occasionally; reduce heat. Cover and simmer 20 minutes. (Do not lift cover or stir.) *8 servings.*

*Mexican Rice with Peas:* Prepare Mexican Rice; stir in 1 cup cooked green peas.

# Pinto Beans
## (Frijoles)

4 cups water
1 pound dried pinto or black beans (about 2 cups)
1 medium onion, chopped (about 1/2 cup)
1/4 cup vegetable oil
2 cloves garlic, crushed
1 slice bacon
1 teaspoon salt
1 teaspoon cumin seed

Mix water, beans and onion in 4-quart Dutch oven. Cover and heat to boiling; boil 2 minutes. Remove from heat; let stand 1 hour.

Add just enough water to beans to cover. Stir in remaining ingredients. Heat to boiling; reduce heat. Cover and boil gently, stirring occasionally, until beans are very tender, about 2 hours. (Add water during cooking if necessary.) Drain; reserve broth for recipes calling for bean broth. Cover and refrigerate beans and broth separately; use within 10 days. *About 6 cups beans and 2 cups broth.*

*Note:* Canned pinto beans can be substituted in recipes calling for Pinto Beans. 1 can (15 ounces) pinto beans, drained, yields about 2 cups.

# Refried Beans
## (Frijoles Refritos)

1/2 cup lard or vegetable oil
2 cups cooked Pinto Beans (opposite)
2 tablespoons chili powder
1 tablespoon ground cumin
1 teaspoon salt
1/8 teaspoon pepper

Heat lard in 10-inch skillet over medium heat until hot. Add Pinto Beans; cook, stirring occasionally, 5 minutes. Mash beans; stir in chili powder, cumin, salt and pepper. Add more oil to skillet if necessary; cook and stir until a smooth paste forms, about 5 minutes. Garnish with shredded cheese if desired. *4 servings.*

*Note:* Canned refried beans can be substituted in recipes calling for Refried Beans. 1 can (17 ounces) refried beans yields about 2 cups.

# Desserts, Sweet Snacks & Beverages

## Sautéed Strawberries
### (Fresas al Coñac)

*½  cup margarine or butter*
*1  quart strawberries, cut into halves*
*¼  cup sugar*
*2  tablespoons orange-flavored liqueur*
*1  teaspoon grated lime peel*
*2  tablespoons brandy*
*Vanilla ice cream*

Heat margarine in 10-inch skillet over medium heat until melted. Add strawberries; cook and stir 1 minute. Stir in sugar, liqueur and lime peel; cook and stir 1 minute. Heat brandy in long-handled saucepan until warm; ignite and pour over strawberries. Serve hot over ice cream. *6 servings.*

## Bananas Flambe
### (Plátanos Flambé)

*4  bananas*
*½  cup margarine or butter*
*¼  cup sugar*
*¼  cup banana-flavored liqueur*
*½  teaspoon ground cinnamon*
*¼  cup brandy*
*Vanilla ice cream*

Peel bananas; cut into ¼-inch slices. Heat margarine in 10-inch skillet over medium heat until melted. Add bananas; cook and stir 1 minute. Stir in sugar, liqueur and cinnamon; cook and stir 1 minute. Heat brandy in long-handled saucepan until warm; ignite and pour over bananas. Serve hot over ice cream. *6 servings.*

*Sautéed Strawberries*

# Pears Stuffed with Dates
## (Peras Rellenas)

¼  cup brandy
1  cup pitted dates
6  pears
2  cups water
⅓  cup sugar
1  stick cinnamon
4  whole cloves
¼  cup grenadine syrup
   Juice of ½ lime (about 2 tablespoons)

Pour brandy over dates; let stand 2 hours. Pare and core pears (do not remove stems). Heat water, sugar, cinnamon and cloves in 3-quart saucepan, stirring occasionally, to boiling; reduce heat and add pears. Simmer uncovered, turning occasionally, until pears are soft but not mushy when pierced with a sharp knife, about 5 minutes. Remove pears with slotted spoon; cool.

Simmer syrup until reduced to ½ cup. Remove cinnamon and cloves. Stir in grenadine and lime juice. Fill pear cavities with dates. Place pears in serving dishes. Spoon about 2 tablespoons syrup onto each pear. Refrigerate until cold, at least 3 hours. *6 servings.*

# Guava Paste and Cream Cheese
## (Ate de Guayaba con Queso)

Cut 1 package (3 ounces) cream cheese into fourths. Cut 4 ounces guava paste into 8 thin slices. Place each piece cream cheese between 2 slices guava paste. Serve with cookies. *4 servings.*

# Fruit Compote
## (Macedonia de Frutas)

1  pineapple
2  cups sugar
2  cups water
1  stick cinnamon
6  whole cloves
3  pears, cut into fourths
3  apples, cut into fourths
3  peaches, cut into fourths
1  tablespoon grated lime peel
¼  cup lime juice

Remove top from pineapple; cut pineapple into fourths. Cut skin and eyes from pineapple. Cut each fourth into ½-inch slices.

Mix sugar, water, cinnamon and cloves in 4-quart Dutch oven. Heat to boiling; stir in pineapple and remaining ingredients. Heat to boiling; reduce heat. Cover and simmer 10 minutes. Remove from heat; allow to cool. Cover and refrigerate until cold. *8 servings.*

---

### ABOUT MEXICAN DESSERTS

The original dessert in Mexican cuisine was fresh fruit such as pineapple, oranges, strawberries, mangoes, papaya, bananas and melons, which grow in abundance. With the introduction of sugar cane into Mexico, a variety of puddings, custards and pastries flavored with cinnamon, almond, caramel, fruit or cheese became popular. Invented or adapted from French and Spanish desserts by Spanish nuns in Peru and Mexico, they were eaten in celebration of feast days. Today, small servings are often served at the end of a meal and more often are eaten between meals. Almond Torte is frequently served as a wedding cake in the Yucatan while Flan is a nation-wide favorite with recipes varying from region to region. Other desserts are pastries like the deep-fried *buñuelos* and *sopaipillas.* Camomile tea or Mexican coffee, *café de olla,* is considered the perfect ending to a Mexican meal.

# Oranges and Cinnamon
## (Naranjas a la Canela)

Pare and thinly slice 4 large chilled oranges. Arrange each orange on crushed ice on individual serving dishes. Just before serving, sprinkle each serving with ¼ teaspoon ground cinnamon and 2 tablespoons coconut. *4 servings.*

# Cognac Custard
## (Flan al Coñac)

¾   cup sugar
2   tablespoons water
½   cup sugar
2   eggs, slightly beaten
2   tablespoons brandy
½   teaspoon vanilla
¼   teaspoon ground nutmeg
¼   teaspoon ground cinnamon
¼   teaspoon ground allspice
    Dash of salt
2   cups milk (scalded then cooled)

Heat ¾ cup sugar in heavy 1-quart saucepan over low heat, stirring constantly, until sugar is melted and golden brown. Gradually stir in water. Divide syrup evenly among six 6-ounce custard cups. Allow syrup to harden in cups about 10 minutes.

Mix ½ cup sugar, the eggs, brandy, vanilla, nutmeg, cinnamon, allspice and salt. Gradually stir in milk. Pour custard mixture over syrup. Place cups in rectangular pan, 13 × 9 × 2 inches, on oven rack. Pour very hot water into pan to within ½ inch of tops of cups.

Bake in 350° oven until knife inserted halfway between center and edge comes out clean, about 45 minutes. Remove cups from water. Refrigerate until chilled; unmold at serving time. *6 servings.*

*Oranges and Cinnamon*

# Mango-Honey Ice Cream
## (Helado de Mango y Miel)

¾  cup sugar
½  cup milk
2  tablespoons honey
2  eggs, beaten
½  teaspoon ground cinnamon
¼  teaspoon salt
½  teaspoon vanilla
2  cups whipping cream
3  cans (15 ounces each) sliced mangoes, drained
    and mashed

Mix sugar, milk, honey, eggs, cinnamon and salt in 2-quart saucepan. Cook over medium heat, stirring constantly, just until bubbles appear around edge. Cool to room temperature. Stir in vanilla, whipping cream and mangoes.

Pour into freezer can; put dasher in place. Cover and adjust crank. Place can in freezer tub. Fill freezer tub ⅓ full of ice; add remaining ice alternately with layers of rock salt (6 parts ice to 1 part rock salt). Turn crank until it turns with difficulty.

Drain water from freezer tub. Remove lid; take out dasher. Pack mixture down; replace lid. Repack in ice and rock salt. Let stand to ripen several hours. *2 quarts ice cream.*

---

### ABOUT MANGOS

The mango is cultivated in the warm climates· of California, Mexico and Hawaii. They are either rounded in shape or elongated and flattened. They vary in color from green to a reddish tinge and have brilliant, orange-yellow pulp. A ripe mango yields to gentle pressure of the fingers. If it is firm to the touch, allow it to ripen at room temperature; when ripe, store it in the refrigerator.

Mangos are usually eaten raw, and have a sweet but slightly tart flavor, rather like a cross between a pineapple and a peach. They are as juicy as they are flavorful.

To prepare a mango, score the skin in fourths with a knife and peel like a banana. Slice the peeled mango lengthwise just above the seed with a sharp knife.

# Mango Mousse
## (Mousse de Mango)

½  cup sugar
2  envelopes unflavored gelatin
4  eggs
3  egg yolks
2  cups mashed ripe mangoes (about 3 mangoes)
¼  cup brandy
¼  teaspoon almond extract
2  cups whipping cream
    Sweetened whipped cream

Mix sugar and gelatin in 2-quart saucepan. Beat eggs and egg yolks until thick and lemon colored, about 5 minutes. Stir eggs into gelatin mixture. Cook over medium heat, stirring constantly, just until mixture boils. Remove from heat. Stir in mangoes, brandy and extract. Chill just until mixture mounds slightly when dropped from a spoon.

Beat whipping cream in chilled bowl until stiff. Fold mango mixture into whipped cream. Pour into 8-cup mold. Refrigerate until firm. Serve with sweetened whipped cream. Garnish with mango slices if desired. *12 servings.*

*Note:* Mangoes can be blended in the blender on high speed until smooth, about 2 minutes.

*Peach Mousse:* Substitute 1 can (29 ounces) sliced peaches, drained, for the mangoes. Blend peaches in blender on high speed until smooth, about 1 minute. Decrease sugar to ¼ cup.

*Apricot Mousse:* Substitute 1 can (30 ounces) apricot halves, drained, for the mangoes. Blend apricots in blender on high speed until smooth, about 1 minute. Decrease sugar to ¼ cup.

## How to Use a Ripe Mango

*1. Score into fourths.*          *2. Slice peeled fruit lengthwise close to the peel.*

# Mexican Bread Pudding
## (Capirotada)

3   cups fresh bread crumbs (about 4 slices)
1/2  cup margarine or butter, softened
1   cup packed brown sugar
1   cup water
2   teaspoons brandy
1/4  teaspoon ground cinnamon
1/8  teaspoon ground cloves
1   cup shredded Cheddar cheese (about 4 ounces)
1   cup chopped dried apples
1/2  cup raisins
1/2  cup chopped walnuts

Dot bread crumbs with ¼ cup of the margarine. Heat in 300° oven, stirring occasionally, until golden brown, about 20 minutes; cool. Heat brown sugar, water, brandy, cinnamon and cloves, stirring constantly, until sugar is dissolved.

Place 1 cup of the bread crumbs in ungreased round pan, 9 × 1½ inches. Pour ⅓ cup of the syrup over crumbs; sprinkle with cheese. Top with 1 cup of the crumbs; sprinkle with apples, raisins and walnuts. Top with ⅓ cup of the syrup and remaining bread crumbs. Pour remaining syrup over crumbs; dot with remaining margarine.

Bake uncovered in 300° oven until hot and bubbly, about 30 minutes. Let stand 10 minutes before serving. Garnish with sweetened whipped cream if desired. *8 servings.*

---

### ABOUT MEXICAN BEVERAGES

Tequila, probably best known of all Mexican alcoholic drinks, is the fermented sap of the agave or century plant, not of the cactus, as is commonly thought. It is named for a small township, Tequila, where agave is grown in long rows. Most tequila is colorless until aged, when it turns a light gold. Tequila is in many cocktails but is also drunk in the classic way accompanied by salt and lime.

Mexicans also enjoy many non-alcoholic drinks or *refrescos*. These include chocolates, deliciously flavored coffees, teas and fruit beverages. The fermented pineapple drink, *tepache,* is not only used as a beverage but also in cooking.

# Crepes with Caramel Filling
## (Crepas con Cajeta)

   *Caramel Custard (below)*
1   cup all-purpose flour
1   tablespoon powdered sugar
1   teaspoon baking powder
1/2  teaspoon salt
1   cup milk
2   eggs, slightly beaten
1/2  teaspoon vanilla
1/4  cup brandy
2   tablespoons powdered sugar
1/2  teaspoon ground cinnamon

Prepare Caramel Custard. Mix flour, 1 tablespoon powdered sugar, the baking powder and salt; add remaining ingredients except brandy, 2 tablespoons powdered sugar and the cinnamon. Beat with hand beater until smooth. Lightly butter 6- to 8-inch skillet; heat over medium heat until bubbly. Pour scant ¼ cup of the batter into skillet; immediately rotate skillet until thin film of batter covers bottom.

Cook until light brown. Run wide spatula around edge to loosen; turn and cook other side until light brown. Stack crepes, placing waxed paper between each. Keep covered. Spread about 2 measuring tablespoons custard on each warm crepe; roll up. Drizzle each crepe with 1 teaspoon brandy; sprinkle with powdered sugar and cinnamon. *12 crepes.*

### Caramel Custard

Pour 1 can (14 ounces) sweetened condensed milk into 8-inch pie plate. Cover tightly with aluminum foil. Place pie plate in square pan, 9 × 9 × 2 inches, on oven rack. Pour very hot water into pan to within ½ inch of top of pie plate. Cook in 425° oven until thick and golden brown, 1 hour. Carefully remove pie plate from hot water. Remove foil; cool. *1¼ cups.*

# Almond Torte
## (Torta de Almendra)

1 cup toasted blanched almonds
1/4 cup all-purpose flour
5 eggs, separated
1/2 cup sugar
1 tablespoon brandy
1 teaspoon almond extract
   Sweetened whipped cream
   Toasted sliced almonds

Heat oven to 350°. Grease and flour 9-inch spring-form pan. Place almonds and flour in blender container. Cover and blend on high speed until almonds are finely ground.

Beat egg whites in large mixer bowl until foamy. Beat in sugar, 1 tablespoon at a time; continue beating until stiff and glossy. Do not underbeat. Beat in egg yolks, 1 at a time. Beat in brandy and almond extract. Fold in almond-flour mixture.

Pour into pan. Bake until top springs back when touched lightly, about 50 minutes. Serve with whipped cream and almonds. *10 to 12 servings.*

# Fried Bread Puffs
## (Sopaipillas)

2 tablespoons lard or shortening
2 cups all-purpose flour
2 teaspoons baking powder
1 teaspoon salt
2/3 cup lukewarm water
   Vegetable oil

Cut lard into flour, baking powder and salt completely. Sprinkle in water, 1 tablespoon at a time, tossing with fork until all flour is moistened and dough almost cleans side of bowl. Gather dough into a ball. Cover and refrigerate 30 minutes.

Heat oil (1 to 2 inches) to 400°. Roll dough on lightly floured surface into rectangle, 12 × 10 inches. Cut into rectangles, 3 × 2 inches. Fry 3 or 4 rectangles at a time until puffed and golden, turning once, about 2 minutes. Drain on paper towels. *20 fried bread puffs.*

# Fried Sweet Puffs
## (Buñuelos)

1/2 cup water
2 tablespoons packed brown sugar
1 egg, slightly beaten
2 tablespoons margarine or butter
2 cups all-purpose flour
1/2 teaspoon baking powder
1/4 teaspoon salt
   Vegetable oil
   Sugar
   Cinnamon
   Honey

Heat water and brown sugar in 1-quart saucepan to boiling; boil uncovered 2 minutes. Cool; stir in egg. Cut margarine into flour, baking powder and salt until mixture resembles fine crumbs; stir in egg mixture. Turn dough onto lightly floured surface. Knead until elastic, 5 minutes. Shape dough into roll, 20 inches long. Cover and let rest 1 hour.

Heat oil (1 inch) to 365°. Cut dough into 1-inch slices. Roll each slice on lightly floured surface into 5-inch circle. Fry circles, turning once, until golden brown, about 2 minutes. Drain on paper towels. Sprinkle with sugar and cinnamon or serve with honey. *20 fried sweet puffs.*

# Fresh Fruit Frappé
## (Trolebús de Frutas)

1 cup cut-up watermelon
1 cup cut-up cantaloupe or honeydew melon
1 cup cut-up pineapple
1 cup cut-up mango
1 cup strawberry halves
1 cup orange juice
1/4 cup sugar

Mix all ingredients. Fill blender container 1/2 full of mixture; fill to top with crushed ice. Cover and blend on high speed until uniform consistency. Repeat with remaining mixture. Serve immediately; garnish with fruit if desired. *7 servings (about 1 cup each).*

*Top: Fresh Fruit Frappé, Bottom: Fried Sweet Puffs*

# Flaming Coffee
## (Café Diablo)

Mexican Coffee (page 89)
¼  cup brandy
   Whipped cream
4  tablespoons coffee flavored liqueur

Prepare Mexican Coffee; keep hot. Heat brandy just until warm in small long-handled pan; ignite and pour flaming over coffee. Pour coffee into 4 individual heatproof glasses or cups. Top each with whipped cream and one tablespoon liqueur. Garnish with cinnamon if desired. *6 servings (about ⅔ cup each).*

# Pineapple Jack
## (Tepache)

1  medium pineapple
6  cups water
6  cups water
1  cup barley
1  stick cinnamon
4  whole cloves
1  package (2 pounds 8 ounces) brown sugar
     (3½ cups packed)
2  cups water

Pare pineapple; reserve peel. Chop pineapple and core. Place pineapple, core, peel and 6 cups water in large glass bowl or crock. Let stand 48 hours.

Heat 6 cups water, the barley, cinnamon and cloves to boiling; reduce heat. Cover and cook until barley is tender, about 1 hour; drain and rinse under running cold water. Stir barley, brown sugar and 2 cups water into pineapple mixture. Let stand 48 hours. Strain through cheesecloth and refrigerate until cold. Serve over ice if desired. *10 servings (about 1 cup each).*

*Flaming Coffee*

## Mexican Tea Punch
## (Ponche de Té)

2  cups tequila
2  cups strong tea
1  cup pineapple juice
¼  cup honey
¼  cup water
   Juice of 1 lemon (about ¼ cup)
   Juice of 1 lime (about ¼ cup)
1½  teaspoons ground cinnamon
1½  teaspoons angostura bitters

Mix all ingredients; refrigerate until cold. Stir before serving. Serve over rice. *12 servings (about ½ cup each).*

## Tamarind Cooler
## (Refresco de Tamarindo)

Cover 1 package (16 ounces) cleaned whole tamarinds with water. Let stand 1 hour. Drain and rinse several times. Place tamarinds in 3 quarts water. Let stand 4 hours. Drain; reserve liquid.

Press as much tamarind pulp through sieve or food mill as possible. Mix reserved liquid, the pulp and 1½ to 2 cups sugar. Cover and refrigerate until chilled. Serve over ice if desired. *8 servings (1 cup each).*

## Camomile Tea
## (Té de Manzanilla)

Pour 4 cups boiling water over 2 tablespoons camomile flowers or tea in heatproof container. Cover and let stand 5 minutes. Stir and strain. *6 servings (⅔ cup each).*

## Rice Beverage Yucatan Style
## (Horchata)

½  cup water
2  tablespoons uncooked regular rice
½  cup water
2  tablespoons ground toasted almonds
2  cups water
⅓  cup sugar
1  teaspoon vanilla
¼  teaspoon ground cinnamon
   Dash of ground cloves
⅛  teaspoon almond extract

Mix ½ cup water and the rice. Mix ½ cup water and the almonds. Let stand 1 hour. Pour rice and water into blender container. Cover and blend on high speed 1 minute; strain. Pour almonds and water into blender container. Cover and blend on high speed 1 minute; add to rice liquid. Add remaining ingredients, stirring until sugar is dissolved. Refrigerate until cold. Serve over ice. *6 servings (about ½ cup each).*

## Mexican Coffee
## (Café de Olla)

½  cup packed brown sugar
6  cups warm water
½  cup regular grind coffee
1  tablespoon camomile tea
½  ounce unsweetened chocolate
2  whole cloves
2  tablespoons ground cinnamon
½  teaspoon vanilla

Heat brown sugar in 3-quart saucepan over low heat, stirring constantly, until sugar is melted. Remove from heat; gradually stir in water. (If sugar should harden, it will dissolve during cooking.) Stir in coffee, tea, chocolate, cloves and cinnamon. Heat to boiling; reduce heat. Simmer uncovered 15 minutes. Stir in vanilla; strain coffee through 2 thicknesses of cheesecloth. *8 servings (½ cup each).*

# Wine Cooler
## (Sangria)

1   bottle (⁴/₅ quart) dry red wine, chilled
½   cup brandy
½   cup orange-flavored liqueur
½   can (6 ounce size) frozen lemonade concentrate,
       thawed (about ⅓ cup)
     Juice of 1 orange (about ⅓ cup)
     Juice of 1 lemon (about ¼ cup)
2   cups ginger ale, chilled

Mix all ingredients except ginger ale; refrigerate.
Just before serving, stir in ginger ale. Garnish with
fruit if desired. *16 servings (½ cup each).*

# Chartreuse Cocktail
## (Romerita)

For each serving, pour 3 parts tequila, 2 parts
green chartreuse and 1 part lime juice over ice in
cocktail shaker; shake until very cold. Garnish with
slice of lime if desired.

*Wine Cooler, Chartreuse Cocktail, Pineapple-Coconut Drink and Lemonade*

# Pineapple-Coconut Drink
## (Piña Colada)

2  *parts light rum*
2  *parts pineapple juice*
1  *part cream of coconut*
   *Crushed ice*

For each serving, place all ingredients in blender container. Cover and blend on high speed until frothy, about 30 seconds. Garnish with fruit if desired.

# Lemonade
## (Limonada)

1½  *cups water*
 1  *cup sugar*
½  *cup lemon juice*
 1  *lime, cut into halves and seeds removed*

Place all ingredients in blender container. Cover and blend on high speed until frothy and lime is coarsely chopped; strain. Serve over ice. *3 servings (about ¾ cup each).*

# GENERAL INDEX

## A

**Almond(s),**
Cauliflower with, Avocado-
Sauce, 74
Chicken Almendrado, 47
Torte, 86
Ancho, 6
Anise seed, 6
**Appetizers,**
see also: Dips
Avocado and Crab, Stuffed, 20
Cheese, Baked, 18
Chilies with Cheese, 18
Chips with Cheese, 13
Corn and Onion Fritters, 15
Crab and Avocado Cocktail, 18
Cucumber Wedges, 13
Eggs, Mexican Deviled, 15
Ham and Cheese, 15
Jicama, 13
Meat and Vegetables, Cold, 18
Meatballs in Chili Sauce, 15
Mushrooms, Stuffed, 16
Oysters, Stuffed, 16
Peanuts in Chile, 14
Peppers Stuffed with Tuna, 21
Plantain Chips, 13
Shrimp Cocktail, Mexican
Style, 21
Tacos, Fried Rolled, 14
Apricot Mousse, 84
Artichoke Hearts, Mustard, 69
**Avocado(s), 8**
About, 20
Cauliflower with, -Almond
Sauce, 74
and Crab Cocktail, 18
and Crab, Stuffed, 20
Dip, 17
and Raisin Dip, 18
and Raisin Dressing, 62
Soup, 27

## B

Baked Cheese, 18
Baked Red Snapper, 43
Baked Stuffed Tomatoes, 76
Bananas Flambé, 81
Basic Green Sauce, 64
Basic Red Sauce, 65
Basil, 6
Bass, Sea in Cilantro, 43
Batter, Corn, 75

**Bean(s)**
About, 24
and Garlic Dip, 17
Green, 76
Pinto, 79
Pinto, Dip, 17
Pinto, Salad, 62
Refried, 79
Sandwiches, Broiled, 36
Soup, 24
**Beef,**
see also Ground Beef
Broth, 26
Burritos, 34
Flank Steak, Stuffed, 50
Meat, Minced, 51
and Plantains, 49
Pot Roast, Mexican, 49
Steak, Broiled, 50
and Tequila Stew, 51
Beer and Cheese Soup, 23
Bell Peppers, 8
**Beverage(s),**
Chartreuse Cocktail, 91
Coffee, Flaming, 88
Coffee, Mexican, 89
Frappé, Fresh Fruit, 86
Lemonade, 91
Mexican, About, 85
Pineapple-Coconut Drink, 90
Pineapple Jack, 88
Punch, Mexican Tea, 89
Rice, Yucatan Style, 89
Tamarind Cooler, 89
Tea, Camomile, 89
Wine Cooler, 90
Black Beans, 8
Braised Meat Loaf, 53
Bread Pudding, Mexican, 85
Bread Puffs, Fried, 86
Broiled Bean Sandwiches, 36
Broiled Steak, 50
**Broth,**
Beef, 26
Chicken, 26
Hot, 29
**Burritos,**
Beef, 34
Fried, 34
Minced Meat, 34

## C

Cactus, 8
Salad, 60
Cakes,
Torte, Almond, 86
Camomile, 6
Tea, 89
Capers, 6

Caramel,
Custard, 85
Filling, Crepes with, 85
**Carrot(s),**
with Green Grapes, 70
and Potatoes, Mashed, 72
Soup, Cream of, 28
Casera Sauce, 65
**Cauliflower,**
with Avocado-Almond Sauce, 74
-Cheese Bake, 74
and Avocado Salad, 61
Chartreuse Cocktail, 91
Chayote, 8
**Cheese,**
About, 71
Baked, 18
and Beer Soup, 23
Broiled Bean Sandwiches, 36
Cauliflower-, Bake, 74
Chile with Cheese Sauce, 75
Chilies, Stuffed, 41
Chilies with, 18
Chips with, 13
Cream and Guava Paste, 82
Eggplant with, 71
and Ham Appetizer, 15
Red Enchiladas with, 31
**Chicken,**
Almendrado, 47
Broth, 26
Cilantro, 46
Mexican, 47
in Mole Sauce, 46
and Orange Salad, 59
Salad, Mexican, 60
Vegetable Soup, 24
**Chili(es), 53**
Chili II, 53
About, 66
with Cheese, 18
with Cheese Sauce, 75
Green, 7
Peanuts in, 14
Peppers, 6
Powder, 7
Sauce, Meatballs in, 15
Sauce, Stuffed Squid in, 45
Stuffed, 41
Chipotle, 6
Sauce, 53
Sauce, Meatballs in, 53
Chorizo, 8
**Cilantro, 7**
Chicken, 46
and Lime, Zucchini with, 67
and Radish Relish, 67
Sea Bass in, 43
Shrimp, 44
Cinnamon, 7
and Oranges, 83
Coconut-Pineapple Drink, 90

# MEXICAN INDEX